THE BREXIT
TAPES

T0347692

THE BREXIT
TAPES

From the Referendum
to the Second Dark Age

Compiled by leading Brextorian

JOHN BULL

unbound

First published in 2023

Unbound
Level 1, Devonshire House, One Mayfair Place, London W1J 8AJ
www.unbound.com

All rights reserved

© John Bull, 2023
Illustrations © Ollie Mann

The right of Gareth Edwards, writing as John Bull, to be identified as
the author of this work has been asserted in accordance with Section
77 of the Copyright, Designs and Patents Act, 1988. No part of this
publication may be copied, reproduced, stored in a retrieval system, or
transmitted, in any form or by any means without the prior permission
of the publisher, nor be otherwise circulated in any form of binding
or cover other than that in which it is published and without a similar
condition being imposed on the subsequent purchaser.

Cover photographs:
© Ben Shread / Cabinet Office / Open Government Licence, commons.
wikimedia.org/wiki/File:Boris_Johnson_election_infobox.jpg
© Hubertl / Wikimedia Commons / CC BY-SA 4.0, commons.
wikimedia.org/wiki/File:Julius_von_Wiesner_(1838-1916),_Nr._71_bust_
(marble)_in_the_Arkadenhof_of_the_University_of_Vienna-1308.jpg

Text design by PDQ Digital Media Solutions Ltd

A CIP record for this book is available from the British Library

ISBN 978-1-80018-257-8 (limited-edition hardback)
ISBN 978-1-80018-161-8 (hardback)
ISBN 978-1-80018-214-1 (paperback)
ISBN 978-1-80018-162-5 (ebook)

Printed in Great Britain by Clays Ltd, Elcograf S.p.A.
1 3 5 7 9 8 6 4 2

This book is dedicated to my mum, Moira,
and my dad, Mick.

You didn't just tolerate your weird kid who was obsessed
with books. You encouraged him.

And to Diane Duane.

Your books first made my imagination take flight.

With special thanks to Mark Hardwicke for his generous
support of this book.

With immortal love of nature, dedicated to the memory
in support of the...

My name is Bozymandias, King of Kings;
I got Brexit done.

Unknown author. Inscription found on broken statue
pedestal near Chatham, Arrondissement of Kent.

Contents

Part Two: The Songs of Brexit

Introduction

How do you describe a historical resource like the Brexit Tapes? This is a question I have found myself considering many times as an academic and as England's official Brextorian, a role I have held since October 3597. It was also the question that immediately jumped into my mind when the TayTay Institute of Social Media asked if I would consider compiling this collection and writing its introduction.

So I will begin by telling you, the reader, the same thing that I tell my students: the Brexit Tapes are history as it happened. Not history as you'll see on a mindstream. Not history as you'll read it in *The Book of Mogg* or hear it in *The Ballads of Grayling*. Not even history as portrayed in Lord Johnson's *Res Brexitica*, still often cited as if it is an official history of that tumultuous time.

That last point is the one that normally causes eyebrows to shoot up in my lectures, but it is also true. Our understanding of this critical point in our history, before the Second Great Plague, before the Second Civil War and before the fracture of the United Kingdom, has long been faulty.

This is nobody's fault. It is simply the result of a problem that has faced historians since the time of Herodotus: what sources can one trust? Our ancestors believed that Hadrian's Wall was built by the Emperor Severus because the Venerable Bede said it was. So it has been with Brexit, where our own understanding of events has been coloured by the writings of the less-than-venerable Lord Johnson and his predecessor, Lady May of Slough.

We can, perhaps, take comfort in the knowledge that for over a millennium our ancestors suffered the same failures of historical understanding as ourselves. Yet our belief that Brexit represented a brief period of strong and stable government (following a period of chaos under Ed Miliband) was a misunderstanding, nonetheless. One that the discovery, fifty years ago, of the first cache of the recordings now known as the Brexit Tapes allowed us to finally address.

This is because the tapes are that rarest of things from the pre-Civil War period: an unedited primary source. The destruction of the National Archives by the Legion Francois during the battle of

Kensington, the Moggist book-burnings and the internet purges undertaken by resurgent Trumpist forces in America ushered in a second Dark Age. Today, well over a thousand years later, our knowledge of that period remains frustratingly limited. Into this darkness, the Brexit Tapes shine a small light.

So let us return to the original question: what are the Brexit Tapes? To answer more prosaically, they are a series of recordings made during the critical Brexit years by two of the prime ministers who governed at the time: Theresa (later Lady) May and Boris (later Lord) Johnson. How they were made we do not know. That it involved some resort to eldritch means – in fact perhaps the first publicly known instance of a British government doing so – seems certain. This is because in addition to standard audio recordings taken from secret microphones in Westminster, they include conversations carried out far outside the circles of government and even the contents of private eldritch thinkspaces. The method is far less interesting, however, than the contents. For they are an unadulterated insight into political decision-making, or sometimes the lack of it, at the time.

Given the sometimes explosive nature of these contents, it is perhaps surprising that any copies of them survived to reach us at all. That they have seems to be thanks to one man: John Bull. Little is known about Mr Bull. Archival scraps suggest that a Captain J. Bull fought with the 1st Walthamstow Irregulars at the Battle of Lea Bridge and during the siege of Soho. Social-media archaeology by the TayTay Institute suggests it is likely the same man. Certainly, the fact the largest hoard of tapes was hidden on a deliberately mislabelled Rick Astley record in the jukebox of Bradley's Spanish Bar in Soho lends force to this argument. Research in this area is ongoing.

Indeed, I must express my personal thanks to the government of New Hanseatic London for letting me see many of the originals, now held in their own archive, while pulling together this compendium. The relationship between the Free Cities and England may currently be peaceful, but, as always, tensions remain. Our shared history, however, points to a time when perhaps the landward gates of London will be thrown open permanently once again.

How Bull came into possession of these recordings remains frustratingly unclear. All we know for certain is that as the political situation deteriorated, he attempted to preserve them for the future by hiding them in plain sight. Along with the Soho hoard, smaller caches have so far been found in the Cambridge computer museum, mislabelled as *Goat Simulator: Hard Copy* and hidden in the BBC Radio 2 sound archive in the Grand Republic of Manchester, labelled as *Steve Wright's Funniest Moments*. This suggests there may be more discoveries yet to come.

For this collection, however, I have limited my selections to elements from that very first discovery: the Soho hoard. This isn't simply because it represents the point at which our understanding of England's history, and that history itself, began to change. It is also because the recordings cover many of the critical moments in the Brexit process, from Lady May's brief time in Downing Street to the early days of Lord Johnson's reign. They are also the only ones for which we have the benefit of Bull's own transcripts.

The selection included here is intended to provide both the general reader and new students of Brextory with a primer to the subject. Where necessary, I have tried to include footnotes giving historical context for the events covered. The TayTay institute have also been kind enough to include a selection of popular Brexit ballads from the time as an appendix.

Taken together, the tapes and ballads included here will hopefully provide you, the reader, with a better knowledge of the events that precipitated the end of the United Kingdom, and the civil war that followed in their aftermath. It may not be history as you've been taught, but it *is* history as it actually happened.

As the events of the tumultuous twenty-first century so effectively demonstrated, accepting the latter is much more important than believing the former.

Mark Hardwicke
Official Brextorian to the Court of St James
November 3613

PART ONE
THE BREXIT TAPES

CHAPTER ONE

FIRST ONE'S GONE...

On 15 November 2018, Prime Minister Theresa May agreed provisional terms with EU negotiators and published a draft Withdrawal Agreement. As many had forecast, this triggered a series of resignations that threatened to bring down her government.

———————————

[Downing Street]

DAVID
LIDINGTON: Our first minister has resigned.
               It's Shailesh.

THERESA MAY: Who?

LIDINGTON: You know... Shailesh. Shailesh Vara.

MAY: David, I was up until four in the
               morning pretending to give a shit
               about Jeremy Corbyn's* recipe for
               raspberry jam. My brain is broken,
               and I have not yet had coffee.
               Who is that?

LIDINGTON: Damn. I was hoping you knew. I'll
               look him up.

LIDINGTON: Okay... Shailesh Vara. According to
               Wikipedia, he's from Cambridgeshire.

MAY: Hmmm.

---

* Better known today as a major deity in the Corbynist pantheon, Jeremy Corbyn was indeed a real man. Many of the events covered by the Brexit Tapes happened during the peak of his power, when he assumed the position of leader of the Labour Party. His removal from this position remains central to the Corbynist religion today. Every November, the faithful lead processions calling for his reinstatement, even though both the Labour Party and the United Kingdom no longer exist.

LIDINGTON: And he has a black belt in taekwondo.
               No controversy section, either.

MAY: Really? Are you sure he's one of ours?

LIDINGTON: 'Implemented devastating cuts to
               legal aid.'

MAY: Oh, right. Yeah. He's *definitely* one
               of ours, then.

LIDINGTON: And there goes Raab. We're going to
               need a new Brexit Minister.

MAY: Dom?! That dirty little traitor.

LIDINGTON: Yup. Here's his letter.

MAY: 'I have resigned so I can spend more
               time with an atlas.'[*]

LIDINGTON: Yes. That part was a bit weird.

LIDINGTON: They'll all start going now.

MAY: Who's next do you think? Chris
               Grayling at Transport?[†]

LIDINGTON: Perhaps. Although I suspect
               Grayling will—

MAY: Careful! Remember the curse.

LIDINGTON: The curse?

MAY: If you say his name three times
               he appears.

LIDINGTON: Ah yes. Sorry. Then Andrea Leadsom
               next, I think. Failing that—

CHRIS   <Schplop> Hello![‡]
GRAYLING:

---

[*] Issues with geography would plague Dominic Raab throughout his life. At the height of the
     Moggist uprising in 2028, Raab mistakenly departed for Germany after being appointed
     Count of the Saxon Shore.
[†] Popular anarchist folk hero Chris Grayling appears frequently in the Brexit Tapes.
     Interestingly, it seems to confirm his status as a man hell-bent on smashing the state.
     Although it also raises significant questions as to how much of this was deliberate.
[‡] As with the 'rebel yell' in the first American Civil War, no recordings exist of the sound Chris
     Grayling made when he appeared. Some historians believe that it was a loud popping noise,
     others that it was a sharp hiss. Bull's own notes at this point in the transcript suggest a baser
     sound. They simply say: 'Like a wet fart.'

8

MAY: Gah!

LIDINGTON: I said, 'Failing'!

GRAYLING: That works too! So, what are we
                talking about?

MAY: Go away, Chris.

GRAYLING: Is it Brexit?

LIDINGTON: Go away, Chris.

GRAYLING: Esther McVey gave me a letter to
                hand to you.

MAY: Shit.

GRAYLING: Oh, and are you going to Michael
                Gove's pizza party[*] later?

LIDINGTON: Oh no...

GRAYLING: It's a secret one! Shhhh!

MAY: If Gove resigns, then we're in
                real trouble.

LIDINGTON: We have a more immediate concern:
                Suella Braverman has gone now.

MAY: Oh, come on. You made that name up.

LIDINGTON: I didn't!

MAY: Who's next? Willie Dustice?

LIDINGTON: She's real! She's an under-secretary
                over in the Department for Brexit![†]

MAY: Oh yes, sure. Tell me: has Dwigt
                Rortugal resigned yet?

LIDINGTON: Look! Here! She's on Wikipedia too!

---

[*] Michael Gove was famous for organising conspiracies under the cover of dinner parties.
Pizza was a particular favourite. Nothing stimulates betrayal like a decent stuffed crust.

[†] It may seem odd now to see doubt cast over the existence of Suella Braverman. Readers
must remember that the tradition of appointing Suella Braverman Home Secretary every
Halloween only started after Brexit.

9

MAY: Oh, for fuck's sake.

[Nearby. A Greggs]

GREGGS   Hello, duck! We've not seen you
EMPLOYEE: in a while!

ED MILIBAND: I've been... away.

GREGGs   Well, it's nice to see you again.
EMPLOYEE: What can I get you?

MILIBAND: A bacon butty, please.

GREGGS   Sure. You want ketchup in that?
EMPLOYEE:

MILIBAND: Drown it.

[Downing Street]

MAY: I hear you're planning another
                pizza party.

GOVE: [On the phone] <Dry hissing>

MAY: How do you think I know?

GRAYLING: Hello!

GOVE: <Sound of wet tentacles>

MAY: Yes, well, you shouldn't have told
                him, then, should you?

GOVE: <Death rattle>

MAY: Can I propose an alternative: why not
                become my Brexit Minister?

GOVE: <Ghoulish wail>

MAY: Think about it, Michael: this could be
                your chance to prove everyone wrong...

GOVE: <Wet clicking>

MAY: Brexit Secretary. *Brexit Secretary*.
                They'd have to admire you.

GOVE: <Tentacle slapping>

MAY: They'd have to love you then, Michael.
                The people, they'd have to respect you.

GOVE: <Demonic purr>

[Parliament. The Terrace Café]

RANIL   Prime Minister...
JAYAWARDENA:

MAY: The lasagne, please. And what's the
                dessert of the day?

JAYAWARDENA: No, Prime Minister, it's me.

MAY:*

JAYAWARDENA: It's Ranil Jayawardena? I'm a
                Parliamentary Private Secretary over
                at Justice.

MAY: Nope, still not ringing any bells.

JAYAWARDENA: Okay, well, anyway. Prime Minister! I
                hereby resign as—

MAY: Meh. Join the queue. I'm on lunch.

[Charing Cross. A stationery shop]

REES-MOGG: I say! Fair maiden! Where is the vellum?
                I must write to the 1922 Committee![†]

---

* One of the noticeable features of the surviving Brexit Tapes is just how often discussions
between the key players descended into painful or nervous silence. In this edition, we
have followed the TayTay Institute recommended style. Silences are indicated by an empty
comment from the relevant speaker.

† The 1922 Committee comprised all Conservative backbench MPs and was a key power
broker in the party. Historians have debated the origins of this name. Some suggest it was a
reference to the 1922 General Election, although it is more likely a reference to the time the
hard right wished to take Britain back to.

CHECKOUT WORKER:	Paper? It's over there.
REES-MOGG:	Vellum, sweet child! *Vellum!* One does not use paper when writing to the Twenty-Two!
CHECKOUT WORKER:	Is that like sticky notes, then? They're in that aisle over there.
REES-MOGG:	*Vellum! Vellum!*
CHECKOUT WORKER:	[Sighing] Sir, there's a queue.

[Parliament. Later]

LIDINGTON:	Rees-Mogg's letter is in.
MAY:	Tedious little shit.
LIDINGTON:	Anything from Gove?
MAY:	Well, I feel a growing sense of terror and an overwhelming urge to vomit, so perhaps his human form approaches.
LIDINGTON:	Ah, no, sorry. That was my fault. I forgot to mute Sky News and they're live with Rees-Mogg.
<Click>	
MAY:	Okay, yes, the feeling has passed now.

LIDINGTON:	Andrea Leadsom's giving a speech in the House. She says she's not resigning.
MAY:	Oh, for fuck's sake. Can't one thing go my way today?
LIDINGTON:	Is that not... a good thing?

MAY: No, it isn't, David. Think about it.
                This means we still need to invite
                her to Cabinet meetings.

LIDINGTON: Right. There are rumours circulating
                again about Chris now. I'll go and—

MAY: Grayling. Grayling. Grayling.

GRAYLING: <Schplop> Hello!

LIDINGTON: I was going to call him.

MAY: The curse is quicker. Chris, have you
                been speaking to Gove again?

GRAYLING: Um... No?

MAY: You're covered in ichor, Chris.

GRAYLING: Ah. Okay, then... yes.

MAY: What did Michael say to you?

GRAYLING: He sang a song, straight into my
                brain. It was sweet, like nectar.
                It was sugar, sorrow and power
                intertwined. Through it all, one word
                resolved: 'resign'.

MAY: Oh Jesus. He got to you.

GRAYLING: Also, he gave me pizza.

MAY:

GRAYLING: It was Hawaiian.

MAY: Sweet mercy.

GRAYLING: Anyway, I think this means I
                must resign.

LIDINGTON: Chris, you're a valuable member of the
                team and...

GRAYLING: It's very nice of you to say so,
                David. But I like to think of myself
                as a man of strong conviction and a
                firm mind. And once I've decided on
                something, I stick to—

MAY: Oh, for fuck's sake. You're not resigning, Chris. You don't want to.

GRAYLING: Oh. Really? Righto. Well, glad that's sorted. I'll be off, then.

MAY: I need a decision, Michael. Are you in or out?

GOVE: [On the phone] <Sound of one hand clapping>

MAY: Sorry, but... is that yes, or no?

GOVE: <Unholy shriek>

MAY: Look, Michael, this conversation would be a lot easier if you assumed human form for a few minutes.

GOVE: <Hideous clicking>

MAY: Yes, I know it's your day off, but still.

LIDINGTON: Rehman Chishti has quit now.

MAY: Who are these people?

LIDINGTON: I have no idea.

MAY: I think I need to start reading stuff that's put on my desk before I sign it.

LIDINGTON: Wait... found him. Okay, we made him a trade envoy, apparently.

MAY: I mean, what even is that?

LIDINGTON: Are trade envoys the ones who go helicopter golfing with Prince Andrew?[*]

---

[*] Historians know very little about the life of this elusive royal, other than that he visited a Pizza Express in Woking on 10 March 2001. The surviving royal archives are oddly specific about that.

14

MAY: No, that's cultural ambassadors.

LIDINGTON: Oh yes.

MAY: Hang on, are they the annoying ones
            we send to the hot, humid countries
            we hate visiting?

LIDINGTON: No, that's Liam Fox.[*]

MAY: Ha! Oh yeah.

LIDINGTON: We need to do something to
            stop the rot.

MAY: I could hold a press conference?

LIDINGTON: Do you actually have anything to say?

MAY: Not really. But that hasn't stopped
            me before.

LIDINGTON: Okay, that's arranged then for you.
            What are you going to say?

MAY: Still no idea. I'll just wing it.

LIDINGTON: Okay, well, remember the
            mantra: 'Imagine what David Cameron[†]
            would do...'

MAY: '... and do the exact opposite.'
            Yes, I know. Actually, do you think
            announcing his arrest and execution
            would help?

LIDINGTON: Prime Minister...

MAY: Sorry. Just thinking out loud.

[*] For Liam Fox, see: Chapters 7, 9, 14, 22–26 (inclusive) and 47 in Pam Brown's gargantuan
     work, *Disgraced Conservative Ministers of the 21st Century (Volume 11)*.
[†] The architect of the Great Collapse and fall of the Union, former Prime Minister David
     Cameron would go on to start a successful garden-shed business, and an even more
     successful lobbying one.

CHAPTER TWO

THE DAY AFTER

With her government having survived the night, the prime minister attempted to stem the flow of resignations the next day. This was no easy task, and required deft negotiations with friends and enemies.

[Downing Street]

MAY:	Okay, Michael.
GOVE:	[On the phone] <Eldritch hiss>
MAY:	Yes, we'll see you soon.
LIDINGTON:	He's coming over?
MAY:	As soon as he's got his human skinsuit on.
LIDINGTON:	I'll lock the cat away.
MAY:	Probably for the best. Can you send down to the kitchen for some live mice, too?

GOVE:	It iS GoOd tO SeE YOu AgaiN, PriMe MINIsTeR. On MY DaY oFF.
MAY:	Thanks for coming over, Michael.
GOVE:	It IS Of nOoo CoNSEqUencE.
MAY:	You're very kind to say so.
GOVE:	AlTHOuGh TOdaY IS My DaY oFF.

16

MAY: Yes, I know, you already mentioned that.

GOVE: YoU wiLL bEGiN bY PaYinG hoMAGE.

MAY: Sorry?

GOVE: <Lip smacking> HOmaGE.

MAY: Oh right, of course. Sorry! David! The
              mice, please.

GOVE: <Crunching of small bones> AH! SwEet,
              teNDeR moRSels.

DAVID: Sweet Mother of God...

GOVE: Do I HAve sOME on MY ChIN?

MAY: David, don't stare.

GOVE: [Wiping] HoW EMBarRAssING. i DO
              ApOLOgise.

MAY: Let me come straight to the point.
              Will you be my Brexit Secretary?[*]

GOVE: WeLL, iT iS a SUBJeCt I HaVE
              OPIniONs oN.

MAY: I know.

GOVE: AnD I hAVE aLWAys bEEn LoYal aND trUE
              to mY FriENDs. BeTRAyaL iS NoT iN
              mY NaTUre.

LIDINGTON: I beg your pardon?

GOVE: OKaY, ApART fROM tHAt ONe TiME.

LIDINGTON: Once?

GOVE: Or PErHAps tWIcE.

LIDINGTON: I'm pretty certain we're into double
              digits by now.

MAY: Be nice, David.

GOVE: If i AM To SErvE yOU, tHEn I
              hAVe dEMAnDs.

[*] The position of Secretary of State for Exiting the European Union was created in 2016 to get
Brexit done. It was abolished in January 2020. Brexit was still not done.

17

MAY: Shoot.

GOVE: I wISh to ReNEgoTIaTe tHE TeRMs oF
               YouR wITHDraWAL aGREEmENT.

MAY: Okay, that's tricky, given the time
               available to us. But maybe.

GOVE: AnD A FRee VoTE oN ITs RaTIFICaTIoN
               iN ParlIAMent.

MAY: Keep talking.

GOVE: iN AddITIoN, aN IteM oN mY STeaM
               wISHList* is ON SAle.

LIDINGTON: More mice?

GOVE: ThANk YoU.

MAY: Okay, Michael, I think we can work
               with this.

GOVE: I hAVe OnE FiNAL DemAND. YoU wILL
               dELiVer uNTo mE BoRIS JohNSoN's hEAd
               oN A pLAte.

MAY: That seems fair, and the idea does
               have a certain appeal...

LIDINGTON: Prime Minister! No!

MAY: Goddamnit.

GOVE: aH. ThEn I aM aFRaID I mUSt decLINE.

[Downing Street. A little later]

MAY: Okay, well at least Michael agreed to
               stop actively plotting against me.

LIDINGTON: Until he finishes *Goat
               Simulator*,† at least.

---

*   Steam was a video-game platform created in 2003. Its initial purpose was to improve
    digital distribution, but our ancestors appear to have used it as a way to hoard games
    that they would never play. See Harrison King, *Lists and Lootboxes: Digital Gaming in the
    21st Century*.
†   Digital archaeologists believe this to be a game of ritual significance.

MAY:	Who's next on our begging list?
LIDINGTON:	Penny Mordaunt.
MAY:	And she is?
LIDINGTON:	Secretary of State for International Development.
MAY:	Jesus Christ.
LIDINGTON:	What?
MAY:	Well, it's hardly a 'great office of state', is it? Fine. Show her in.

PENNY MORDAUNT:	Prime Minister, if you want my continued loyalty, then I have demands.
MAY:	You do realise that you're only the International Development Secretary, right?
MORDAUNT:	Sorry?
MAY:	I mean... seriously.
MORDAUNT:	I really don't appreciate your tone here.
MAY:	And I don't appreciate—
LIDINGTON:	Prime Minister...
MAY:	[Sighing] Fine. Go ahead.
MORDAUNT:	I think it's about time I got some respect around here.
MAY:	You know that Gove is still outside, right? If I ask him, he will literally flay your face off? *Michael!*
GOVE:	HeLLo PeNNy.
MORDAUNT:	Keep that... that *thing* away from me!
GOVE:	ThAT iS vErY HurTfuL.

LIDINGTON:	Prime Minister...
MAY:	God. Fine. What do you want, Penny?
MORDAUNT:	I want a free vote on your Withdrawal Agreement.
MAY:	Fine.
MORDAUNT:	And I want people to know that it was my idea.
MAY:	Knock yourself out.
MORDAUNT:	And one more thing — an item on my Steam wishlist is on sale.
GOVE:	iS It *GoAt SImULAtor*?
MORDAUNT:	Oh my God! You've played it?
GOVE:	hONesTLY, It'S sO GoOD.

———————————

[Downing Street. That afternoon]

LIDINGTON:	David Davis[*] is on the radio now.
MAY:	Of course he is.
LIDINGTON:	He says he would have run the EU negotiations differently if he had been in charge.
MAY:	Oh really? Did he remind everyone that he was Brexit Minister for *two years* before I fired him?
LIDINGTON:	No.
MAY:	Funny that.

[*] 'Few men in history have been as consistently wrong as David Davis. For a significant part of the early twenty-first century, the easiest way to be on the right side of history was to make sure David Davis was on the other side of it.' Claire Parker, *These Charmless Men: Male Privilege and Parliament in the Twenty-First Century*

LIDINGTON: The previews of tomorrow's papers
are in as well. Gove is all over
them. He says he's still thinking
of quitting.

MAY: That eldritch little shit. I bought
him *Goat Simulator*.

LIDINGTON: To be fair, it's not that
long a game.

MAY: Am I the only person in the Cabinet
who hasn't been playing this game?

LIDINGTON: It sounds like it.

MAY: I feel so out of touch.

LIDINGTON: Are you not on Ken Clarke's[*] Discord?[†]
It's been all over that. He's been
streaming it for months.

MAY: I left. I got tired of his endless
Fortnite memes.

[Downing Street. That evening]

MAY: So I'm controlling the goat?

KEN CLARKE: [Over Discord] Yes! *Goat Simulator*!
Control it with WASD and try to do as
much damage as you can.

MAY: Why?

CLARKE: Just because you can.

MAY: It's so senseless, though, and it
doesn't actually achieve anything.

CLARKE: But it's fun for the goat.

---

[*] Although best known to history for his nine gold medals at the inaugural Olympic E-Games, Ken Clarke also served as a Conservative MP for almost fifty years. During that time, he built a reputation for pragmatic, thoughtful conservatism and a willingness to put country before party. His attempts to become the leader of the party thus failed.
[†] Discord was a platform designed for online discussion. Nominative determinism was important to our ancestors.

MAY:	I suppose so but... Oh *fuck off*, Ken. I see what you're doing here.
CLARKE:	Who, me?

MAY:	[Logging off] Clarke is a devious old shit, isn't he?
LIDINGTON:	Always has been, always will be. Don't play him at *Fortnite*. He's lethal.
GOVE:	[On TV] i aM LoOkInG ForWARd tO CoNTInuING tO wORk WiTH aLL mY cOlLeAgUes iN GoVERnMEnt.
MAY:	He looks better. Is that a new skinsuit?
LIDINGTON:	He says it gives off less static in wet weather.

[Elsewhere. A darkened room]

ANDREA LEADSOM:	I convene this secret meeting to discuss demanding a renegotiation of the Withdrawal Agreement. Does anyone have any questions?
GRAYLING:	Andrea, is there going to be pizza?
LEADSOM:	No. Anyone else?
GRAYLING:	I have another question.
LEADSOM:	No, Chris. There will not be pizza at the next meeting either.
GRAYLING:	Bugger.
MORDAUNT:	I have a question: Is Gove still on board with this?
LEADSOM:	I believe so. I can feel his presence in my mind.

GOVE: [Ethereal voice] DoN'T mINd mE — i'M
               jUsT LuRKing.

GRAYLING: Ooh! Another question.

LEADSOM: Yes, Chris?

GRAYLING: Have we *definitely* ruled out pizza?

LEADSOM: Okay, to confirm. We will meet again
               this weekend to decide, definitively,
               whether we do this.

GOVE: bUT nOT oN SuNDay, as i'M aT
               RaMBliNG cLUb.

LEADSOM: And, in deference to Chris, there
               will be pizza.

GRAYLING: *Get in!*

MORDAUNT: Last question: are we
               inviting Liam Fox?

LEADSOM: God, do we have to?

GOVE: LeTS nOT. hE CrEEps mE OuT.

CHAPTER THREE

SECRETARY OF STATE FOR BREXIT

Once the initial crisis point had been passed, Theresa May's first challenge was to find a new Brexit Secretary, a role previously held by Dominic Raab. Historical research has shown that few candidates seemed willing to take on the role at the time, as turnover in the position was rather brisk.

[Downing Street]

LIDINGTON: I wonder if we should filter out those who haven't already plotted against us.

MAY: I mean, it would nice.

LIDINGTON: Here's one. What about Margot James?

MAY: Remainer.

LIDINGTON: Damn.

MAY: Anyone else?

LIDINGTON: No, that was pretty much it. We were fishing in a very small pool.

MAY: What about people who've only done it once?

LIDINGTON: That gives us... IDS?[*]

MAY: Fuck off.

---

[*] IDS was a common nickname for Iain Duncan Smith, then the Conservative MP for Chingford. This is not to be confused with IBS (irritable bowel syndrome). One was an uncomfortable, painful, bloated mess. The other was a medical condition.

LIDINGTON: Ah wait, here's one...
               Stephen Barclay.

MAY: Never heard of him.

LIDINGTON: Just looking him up... literally two
               paragraphs on Wikipedia.[*]

MAY: Is one 'controversy'?

LIDINGTON: Nope.

MAY: Then he'll do.

[Westminster. Later that morning]

MAY: Hello Stephen.

STEPHEN: Oh God. What have I done wrong?

MAY: Nothing, Stephen!

STEPHEN: Um... actually, it's Steve. Please
               though, what was it? What did I do?

MAY: No need to be so nervous, Stephen.

STEPHEN: It's just I've never been in Number
               Ten before.

MAY: Really?

STEPHEN: Well, once, but... God, sorry, I'm
               not very good at this stuff.

MAY: [Aside] Oh he's *perfect*.

LIDINGTON: Isn't he just?

MAY: Stephen...

STEPHEN: Steve. Just so you know, I haven't
               written a letter to the 1922
               Committee.

[*] 'Of the many fan-fiction platforms used by our ancestors, Wikipedia appears to have been
     the most common. It offered a mix of fact and fiction that few others could match.' Deirdre
     Tobin, *21st Century Writing: A Wiki Wild Wild West*

MAY:	Pardon?
STEPHEN:	A letter asking for your removal. I don't know what you've heard. But I haven't written to the 1922 Committee.
MAY:	I know, Stephen.
STEPHEN:	Oh *God*, of course you know! Sorry. I'm just...
MAY/STEPHEN:	[Together] Nervous.
STEPHEN:	Hahaha...
MAY:	Yes. Ha.
MAY:	Anyway. Congratulations, Stephen.
STEPHEN:	Steve.
MAY:	Stephen. You're here because I want to *promote* you.
STEPHEN:	Oh God, *please* not Work and Pensions?!
MAY:	Even better!
STEPHEN:	Oh no...
MAY:	Congratulations, Mr Brexit Secretary!
STEPHEN:	*Oh God... Oh God... Oh God... Oh God...* Sorry... Oh God... I just... I can't breathe...
MAY:	It's fine. Take a minute.
STEPHEN:	Oh God... Oh God... Oh God...
MAY:	Do you want a paper bag to breathe into?
LIDINGTON:	Try putting your head between your legs.
STEPHEN:	Oh God... Oh God.... I think I'm going to be sick.
LIDINGTON:	[Pointing] Toilet's that way.
<Vomiting>	

LIDINGTON: So, do we think that went well?

MAY: Sarcasm doesn't suit you, David.

LIDINGTON: Sorry.

MAY: Right. Now that's sorted, get me the
              Chancellor. I need to run through
              the economics of the Withdrawal
              Agreement.[*]

LIDINGTON: You want to talk to Phil Hammond?
              Ah. Right...

MAY: What?

[A *Fortnite*[†] server]

CLARKE: Shouldn't you be doing
              something today?

PHIL HAMMOND: Probably.

CLARKE: You going to?

HAMMOND: Nope.

HAMMOND: Any heals?

CLARKE: Here. Oh hey! David's logged on. I'll
              invite him to join us.

HAMMOND: No! Don't invite him! Don't inv—

LIDINGTON: Hey everyone, what game mode are we...
              Oh. Hi Phil.

HAMMOND: Hi David.

LIDINGTON: You weren't at work this morning.

HAMMOND: I was ill. I sent you a
              text about it.

---

[*] 'What Theresa May spent several years attempting to achieve through diplomacy, Boris
Johnson would later manage by simply changing the font. This did not turn out to be the
clever wheeze he thought it would be.' Richard Abraham, *A Ham-Fisting: The Legacy of Brexit*

[†] Fortnite seems to have been a popular arena sport in which people with short attention
spans fought each other loudly and violently. It has been described as 'the Commons, but
with lootboxes'

CLARKE: Dude knocked at Retail Row. Someone
                 finish him. I need Mats.

LIDINGTON: And you've not answered any of
                 Theresa's emails this afternoon.

HAMMOND: That's because I'm still ill.

LIDINGTON: You don't sound it.

HAMMOND: Really? Must be the mic.

CLARKE: Guys, can we *please* focus on the game.

LIDINGTON: [Sighing] Can we at least invite
                 Stephen in? I want to make him feel
                 part of the team.

HAMMOND: Who?

LIDINGTON: Stephen Barclay.

HAMMOND: That doesn't answer my question.

LIDINGTON: He's the new Brexit Secretary.

HAMMOND: Oh right. I did wonder whose turn it
                 was this week.

CLARKE: Snork.

LIDINGTON: Chaps, please.

HAMMOND: No, seriously, how are you picking
                 Brexit Secretaries these days?

CLARKE: I believe it's the minimum sentence
                 for shoplifting.

LIDINGTON: Gents, it's a serious role, with real
                 responsibility.

HAMMOND: - Oh sure, of course.

CLARKE: That's why David Davis did it for
                 two years.

HAMMOND: And Dominic Raab. A man who thinks
                 Calais is French for a milky coffee.

LIDINGTON: Look, please, can we invite Stephen
                 to join the game?

HAMMOND: I mean, what's the *point* of a Brexit
                Secretary?

CLARKE: [Sighing] Fine. Invited.

STEPHEN: Hey everyone.

PHIL HAMMOND: Stephen.

CLARKE: Stevey!

STEPHEN: Actually, it's Steve. I'm new to this.
                What do I do?

HAMMOND: Stand at the front. Absorb all the
                flak so that we don't.

CLARKE: *Ha!*

LIDINGTON: Phil!

HAMMOND: What?! I'm talking about *Fortnite*!

CHAPTER FOUR

A VERY MOGGY COUP

In the weeks following the Withdrawal Agreement's publication, Theresa May's position remained on a knife-edge. For a brief period, the power to remove her seemed to sit with one person. Cometh the hour, history tells us, cometh the Mogg.

[Downing Street]

MAY: Anything in the morning papers?

LIDINGTON: Rees-Mogg.

MAY: Bless you.

LIDINGTON: No, Jacob Rees-Mogg. He claims that
                the ERG[*] have almost got enough
                letters in to the 1922 Committee to
                trigger a vote of no confidence in
                your leadership of the Tory Party.[†]

MAY: Ha! He said that on Friday too.

LIDINGTON: He seems pretty confident in his
                abilities.

MAY: Well, of course he does. Have you
                ever been to an ERG meeting, David?

LIDINGTON: God, no.

---

[*] The European Research Group (ERG) began as a political pressure group within the Conservative Party. In 2026 they formed the bulk of the members of the short-lived New Parliament, appointed by Rees-Mogg during the Moggist Uprisings.

[†] 'It is a curious oddity that, at a critical time in its history, Britain's future depended not on the competence of the prime minister, but on how many Conservative MPs had easy access to a book of stamps.' Stephen Bonner, *Stamps & Duty: A History of Parliamentary Letters*

MAY: It's like someone liquified some
                  YouTube comments, then injected them
                  into a pile of hams.

[An ERG Meeting. That morning]

JAMES   ... And that's why Doctor Who should
CLEVERLY: go back to being a man.

JACOB   Thank you, James. Most enlightening.
REES-MOGG: Next up, Christopher Chope.* Chris,
                  the floor is yours.

CHOPE: Dear Members, I think it is time
                  that we addressed one of the *great
                  injustices* of our time. I have begun
                  a campaign to create an International
                  Men's Day—

GOVE: ThErE aLReadY is OnE.

CHOPE: Sorry, what?

GOVE: nO, ReALLY. iT's toDaY. InTERNatIONal
                  MeN'S dAY, niNETeeNth oF nOVemBER.

CHOPE: Well, that must be new!

GOVE: hARDly. iT's BEen ArOuND siNCE 1992.

REES-MOGG: Well, that's bloody good work all
                  round! Well done, Chris!

GOVE: iS mY HuMAn vOICE nOt wORKing? I
                  sAId 1992.

REES-MOGG: This is a huge victory for ERG
                  political pressure! Huzzah!

ALL: Huzzah!

GOVE: [Tapping his mouth] iS ThIS ThINg oN?

---

* Later, High Inquisitor Chope of the Moggist forces. Indeed, Chope would die leading the second Moggist invasion of France in 2028. For more information see Ruth Crawford's excellent book, *Lions Led By Gammon: The Bay of Hogs Disaster*.

REES-MOGG: Okay, well I know you're all keen now
                to head off and celebrate the new
                International Men's Day...

GOVE: [Muttering] wHIch is nOt neW.

REES-MOGG: But *please* don't forget to put your
                letters in to the 1922 Committee!
                Hands up everyone who has done so.
                Excellent, excellent, excellent...
                Oh, Chris.

CHOPE: Sorry, Moggy.

REES-MOGG: Okay, let's go through this again. We
                need forty-eight letters, submitted
                to the Committee by Conservative MPs,
                to trigger a vote of no confidence.
                Now get your pens out, and copy
                this down...

CHOPE: Yes, Moggy.

[Downing Street. The same time]

MAY: So, I'm thinking today we come out on
                the attack.

LIDINGTON: Emphasise the problems of a no-
                deal Brexit? Demand an end to the
                unrealistic expectations being
                pushed by various senior Brexiteers?
                I like it.

MAY: Actually, I was just going to blame
                immigrants for a bit. You know, focus
                people back on our shared beliefs.

LIDINGTON: Okay, well that works too.

MAY: Anything else in the papers I should
                be aware of?

LIDINGTON: Well, Greg Clark's now suggesting we
                extend the transition period to 2022.

MAY: Isn't that just punting all the issues
                into the future?

LIDINGTON: Yes. Indeed, it would punt them beyond
                the next election.

MAY: Oooh. Good point.

[An ERG meeting. A little later]

REES-MOGG: So, are we clear now on how these
                letters need to be structured?

CHOPE: Yes, Moggy.

REES-MOGG: Because this is *very* important.
                I cannot emph—

NICE LADY: Hello? Sorry. But we've got the
                community room for Parents and Toddlers
                and you're already ten minutes over.

REES-MOGG: My dear lady! This is important! The
                fate of our country is at stake!

NICE LADY: Then next time book the room for more
                than an hour.

[Somewhere else. A little later again]

REES-MOGG: The *tyranny* of the *Remainer* Cabinet
                must end! *Sovereignty* must return to
                this Sceptred Isle! Our borders must
                be secured!

MUFFLED VOICE: Sir this is a McDonald's Drive Thru.
                You can't park here.

REES-MOGG: *Infamy!*

GOVE: I tHInK TheREs a CoSTA CoFFEe rOUnd
                tHe CoRNeR.

[A Costa Coffee.[*] Still later]

REES-MOGG: As I was saying before, the prime minister will fear our modern knights of the rou—

CHOPE: Moggy, I don't think this tea is served in real china.

REES-MOGG: *Infamy!*

MARK FIELD: Moggy! Look over there! A breast! That woman's breastfeeding! In public!

REES-MOGG: *Horror!*

STEVE BAKER: Moggy, there are a lot of men with laptops in here. Do you think they're MI6?

REES-MOGG: *Outrage!*

GOVE: [To itself] ThIS iS sO MuCH FuN.

———————————

[A staircase in Westminster. That afternoon]

HAMMOND: How was ERG earlier?

GOVE: a wASTeLaND oF ToXIc mASCuLiNitY AnD PriVIleGE, tINGeD wITh zEOlotRY aND mADNess.

HAMMOND: Same as always, then.

STEPHEN: That sounds awful. Why go?

GOVE: eRm, eLdriTCH hOrRor. ReMEmBEr?[†]

STEPHEN: Oh. Oh right.

GOVE: HaVe WE mEt, bY tHe WAy?

HAMMOND: That's Stephen.

---

[*] Coffee shops played an important part in ritual life for our ancestors. An offering was made, in some cases of significant financial value, and a cup of burnt coffee received and drunk. This is presumed to have been a form of daily penance.

[†] Eldritch horrors have been a feature of many British governments. Indeed, the Home Office began recruiting heavily from the eldritch realm in 1979. Gove appears to have been the first to operate openly in Cabinet, however.

STEPHEN:	Steve.
HAMMOND:	He's the new Brexit Secretary.
GOVE:	oH DeAr.
STEPHEN:	Why do people keep saying that?
HAMMOND:	For the same reason that none of us can be bothered to learn your surname. Tick-tock, Stephen. Tick-tock.

HAMMOND:	Okay, Cabinet time. Before we go in, though, I've got something for you, Stephen.
STEPHEN:	Steve.
HAMMOND:	It's a present.
STEPHEN:	Um. It's a shirt. Thanks, I suppose?
HAMMOND:	Do you like it?
STEPHEN:	It's quite bright.
HAMMOND:	Wear it to Cabinet. It's a tradition for Brexit Secretaries.
STEPHEN:	Really? Well... Okay.

MAY:	Okay. First on the agenda today...
GRAYLING:	I have a question!
MAY:	... there's no pizza, Chris.
GRAYLING:	Bugger.
MAY:	First on the agenda is the Withdrawal Agreement. Look, I'm not going to mince words here. This Brexit deal is the be... Oh, *come on*.
CABINET:	<Sniggers>

36

MAY: Honestly, you're like children
            sometimes.

STEPHEN: Why is everyone laughing?

MAY: Own up. Which one of you made Stephen
            wear a red shirt?

[Conservative Party chairman's office. The same time]

REES-MOGG: Party chairman, it is I! Jacob
                Rees-Mogg!

GRAHAM BRADY: Oh God.

REES-MOGG: You know why I'm here, Graham.

BRADY: I do, and it could have been an email.

REES-MOGG: Did Brutus dispatch Caesar via email?

BRADY: I suspect he would have, if he could.

REES-MOGG: Enough frivolity. Tell me, good man,
                tell me of the forty-eight letters!

BRADY: Twenty-seven.

REES-MOGG: What?

BRADY: Wait... actually, twenty-six. I'm
                pretty certain Grant Shapps[*] has
                put two in.

REES-MOGG: Oh.

BRADY: Sorry, Jacob.

REES-MOGG: Could you perhaps re-count?

BRADY: What?

REES-MOGG: Re-count them. In case some got
                stuck together.

BRADY: I haven't missed twenty
                letters, Jacob.

---

[*] Of the various eldritch beings to operate in the government, Shapps seems to have been the only gestalt entity. One who often appears in our records under several different names.

REES-MOGG: But I don't understand. I spoke to
loads of MPs and they all promised...[*]

BRADY: Jacob, I don't mean to be cruel,
but have you thought about getting a
different hobby?

---

[*] 'When Rees-Mogg raised his banner in Oxford, Mark Francois was one of the first to answer the call. He was duly rewarded with high command. One suspects the Moggist kingdom would have lasted longer had this not been the case.' Matt Kilcast, *A Little Short for a Stormtrooper: Moggist Strategy Under Mark Francois*

CHAPTER FIVE

THE MIRACLE OF DUNQUACK

After the threat of a no-confidence vote had passed, attention turned to the practicalities of Theresa May's Withdrawal Agreement. Two things quickly drew attention: the need for some way of managing cross-border traffic in Ireland, and the lack of cross-Channel ferry capacity during the transition period. The prime minister released a 'political declaration', claiming it would provide some clarity on both matters.

[In Westminster]

MAY: Ah. You're reading my latest political
            declaration!* What do you think?

LIDINGTON: Well, it doesn't really say or promise
            anything new, does it?

MAY: Thanks.

LIDINGTON: I see 'technology' will apparently
            solve the Irish border problem now.

MAY: Yes. In fact, I wanted to talk to you
            about that. I need you to find us a
            software developer.

LIDINGTON: Um... really? Are you sure?

MAY: What's the problem?

---

* 'Lady May of Slough seems to have been particularly fond of political declarations. So were her enemies. They allowed them to work out how she was going to fail next, well in advance.' Paula Claytonsmith, *Political Rivalry and the Fall of Britain*

LIDINGTON: Nothing, I'm just... well, surprised
              you trust me to organise something
              like that after last time.

MAY: Last time?

[Flashback to September 2018]

LIDINGTON: So I hired a presentation-skills tutor
              for you, like you asked.

MAY: Brilliant.

LIDINGTON: He should be here any min—

MR BLOBBY: [Bursting into the room] BLOBBY
              BLOBBY BLOBBY!

MAY: What the fuck?! *Get it off me!*

LIDINGTON: [Trying to fight Blobby off] It said
              Noel's House Party star! I thought it
              would be Noel!

MAY: *How would that have been any better?*

[Back in November 2018]

MAY: Well, yes. I've still not forgiven
              you for the Blobby thing.

LIDINGTON: I honestly cannot tell you how
              terribly sorry I am about that.

MAY: But I don't really have a choice.
              I'm not exactly blessed with 'team
              players' right now. I've even
              had to ask Chris to sort out the
              cross-Channel ferry problem, for
              fuck's sake.

LIDINGTON: You've what?

40

[The Department for Transport. The same time]

GRAYLING: Right, chaps! Thank you all for coming. So, the prime minister says we're in charge of freight shipping! Which is *terribly* exciting.

CIVIL SERVANT: Okay, sir. Well, in that case we'll need to look at sourcing additional ferries and—

GRAYLING: Oh God, no. I think we need to be more digital than that. Think outside the box.

POLITICAL ADVISOR: Great idea, Minister.

GRAYLING: Thank you.

CIVIL SERVANT: I'm sorry, what? I don't understand.

GRAYLING: It's like 'the Digital Railway'.[*]

CIVIL SERVANT: But that doesn't really mean anything.

POLITICAL ADVISOR: People do love digital.

CIVIL SERVANT: Because they don't know what it means.

POLITICAL ADVISOR: Exactly! It's just nice and... futuristic.

GRAYLING: Let's call this... Dunkirk 2.0!

CIVIL SERVANT: You what?

POLITICAL ADVISOR: Dunkirk 2.0? That's inspired, sir.

GRAYLING: Thank you.

---

[*] Like overhead electrification in the north of England, the Digital Railway is something that remains unimplemented today.

CIVIL SERVANT:	But... but what does that phrase even mean?!
GRAYLING:	It means... well, Dunkirk, isn't it?
POLITICAL ADVISOR:	It means taking back control!
GRAYLING:	Exactly!
POLITICAL ADVISOR:	It means brave little British ships!
GRAYLING:	Huzzah!
CIVIL SERVANT:	Oh my God, this is a madhouse.
POLITICAL ADVISOR:	Do we have any little ships, though? They might be expensive to buy.
GRAYLING:	That's a good point.
CIVIL SERVANT:	This conversation is insane.
GRAYLING:	Thinking even further outside the box... do we really *need* them?
POLITICAL ADVISOR:	Hmm. We could block-book Eurostar instead?
CIVIL SERVANT:	What?!
GRAYLING:	Oh, I like that. It's digital *and* railway!
CIVIL SERVANT:	What are you both talking about?! This isn't about making sure people can still pop over to Paris for the weekend! We need to move goods. That means we need the little ships and... Oh my God, why am I now the one defending the little ships thing?!

[A Whitehall interview room. A little later]

LIDINGTON: So, looking at your CV, it says here that you do Java, C++ and something called '.Net'?

SOFTWARE
DEVELOPER:

LIDINGTON: I'm a bit of a computer whiz myself, you know. Excel macros.

SOFTWARE
DEVELOPER:

LIDINGTON: Even did an HTML course once.

SOFTWARE
DEVELOPER:

LIDINGTON: Ahem... Anyway, thank you for coming in for an interview. Let's begin. Question one: How would you use technology to solve the Irish border?

SOFTWARE   Sorry, what did you just say? You
DEVELOPER: want me to tell you how I would 'solve' the Irish border?

LIDINGTON: Yes. No need for specifics right now. Just tell me how long it will take and how much it will cost.

SOFTWARE   But... that's impossible! I mean,
DEVELOPER: I'd need *far* more information to scope this.

LIDINGTON: No problem. I completely understand.

SOFTWARE   Thank God.
DEVELOPER:

LIDINGTON: I've got a name for it and I've designed a logo, so I can share those, too.

SOFTWARE
DEVELOPER:

LIDINGTON: And if you can show me some designs for it, I could tell you what I *don't* like about them?

SOFTWARE DEVELOPER: This isn't how software or systems development works. I can build something to implement a business process, but...

LIDINGTON: Hey! Easy there, tiger! I'm not asking for details. I just want a technical solution to the Irish border. I don't need to know the specifics of how it should work.

SOFTWARE DEVELOPER: But *I* need to know the specifics of how it should work!

LIDINGTON: Isn't that the bit technology deals with?

SOFTWARE DEVELOPER: No!

LIDINGTON: Okay, well how about we approach this a different way. Could you just give me a ballpark figure?

SOFTWARE DEVELOPER: No, because you still haven't defined the problem.

LIDINGTON: Well, the problem is the Irish border, obviously.

SOFTWARE DEVELOPER: Yes, but what's the business process you want me to implement to deal with that?

LIDINGTON: You don't need business processes if you have technology.

SOFTWARE DEVELOPER: Yes! You do!

LIDINGTON: Oh, also I have a note from Matt Hancock.[*] He suggests we use something called 'blockchain' for this. Apparently he read about it in *Wired*.

SOFTWARE DEVELOPER: I don't have nearly enough information to quote for this.

LIDINGTON: I don't see why it's so hard. I've given you some ideas and a logo.

SOFTWARE DEVELOPER: That's not enough.

LIDINGTON: Oh also, I should probably mention that we don't have a big budget for this.

SOFTWARE DEVELOPER: What?

LIDINGTON: It'll be great exposure, though. I'll recommend you to people.

SOFTWARE DEVELOPER:

LIDINGTON: And we need it by March.

[The Department for Transport. The same time]

GRAYLING: So you're insisting on ships, then? That seems awfully backward.

CIVIL SERVANT: Yes! And a few big ones at that. Proper ferries. The logistics of that will be hard enough.

GRAYLING: Oh piffle. I play with boats in my bath at home all the time. It's not that hard.

---

[*] For centuries, *Pandemic Diaries: The Inside Story of Britain's Battle Against Covid* by Matt Hancock was believed to be one of the finest political satires of all time. The discovery of the Brexit Tapes provided the first concrete evidence that it was not a fictional work by an anonymous author. Astonishingly, modern scholarship has confirmed that Matt Hancock really did exist, and held the position of Secretary of State for Health far longer than common sense would seem to dictate.

CIVIL SERVANT:	That's not the same thing.
GRAYLING:	And a rubber duck. Oh wait. Now that's an idea...
CIVIL SERVANT:	Please, no.
GRAYLING:	No, bear with me, I think I'm having an epiphany. So... have we *completely* ruled out the option of using a couple of giant ducks instead?
POLITICAL ADVISOR:	I like that. Very outside the box.
CIVIL SERVANT:	Giant. Ducks.
POLITICAL ADVISOR:	Giant ducks would be very eco-friendly too. That's big at the moment.
CIVIL SERVANT:	Someone make this stop...
GRAYLING:	Or... what about a whole *fleet* of regular-sized ducks?
POLITICAL ADVISOR:	A duck cloud! That's *very* digital.
GRAYLING:	Exactly. Well, there it is, gentlemen, I believe we have a plan.

[Downing Street. That afternoon]

MAY:	So how did it go with the software developer?
LIDINGTON:	Not good. She kept whining about processes and workflows.
MAY:	Bloody techies. This is why I hate small development firms. Too many questions. Why can't they just get on with it?

LIDINGTON: I know.

MAY: Guess it's time to ring round
               the regulars.

LIDINGTON: Hello, so we have a large IT
               project and...

PACITA GUY:*   [On the phone] It wILl bE thIrTY-
               niNe bILLiOn aNd thAT dEAdLINe is nOT
               a ProBLEm.

LIDINGTON: Oh great, thanks. That's...
               wait! I haven't told you what we
               actually need yet!

PACITA GUY: oH gOd, I fORgot. SoRRy, yES.
               YoU gO FiRSt.

LIDINGTON: So you're sure you can do this?

PACITA GUY: oH yEs. sCOTtiSH bORder. ThiRtY-niNe
               BilLioN. MaRCh. YoU haVE a LogO.
               nO PrOBLem.

LIDINGTON: Irish border.

PACITA GUY: iRiSH. YeS. ThAT's WhaT I sAID.

LIDINGTON: You didn't. You said Scottish.

PACITA GUY: nO i diDN't.

LIDINGTON: Look, you sound awfully familiar.
               Have we met?

PACITA GUY: nO, bUt I dO hAVe a bROthER.

---

* Unfortunately, the tapes are corrupted at this point and the name of the IT company with
which the government regularly dealt has been lost to time. Our use here represents current
thinking on its likely identity.

[The Treasury. The same time]

CIVIL
SERVANT: Purchase order from the Department
             for Transport, sir. I think...
             well, I think you may want to look
             at this one.

HAMMOND: Oh God, is it another locksmith?
             Has Chris locked himself in the
             toilet again?

CIVIL
SERVANT: No, sir. Here.

HAMMOND: [Reading] Oh, for the love of... Hand
             me the fucking phone.

GRAYLING: [On the phone] Hello!

HAMMOND: *Forty-eight thousand ducks?!*

GRAYLING: Operation Dunquack!

CHAPTER SIX

HMS *ROGAL DORN*

Defence Secretary Gavin Williamson was a keen, long-time supporter of the military. With the prime minister and Treasury focused on economic impact forecasts for Brexit, he was given the freedom to take a more hands-on approach to the department's operational management than previous office holders.

———————

[The Ministry of Defence]

GAVIN
WILLIAMSON: Okay. So, I've looked at the list of names for the first of our new class of submarines.

FIRST SEA
LORD: I see, Minister.

WILLIAMSON: And I have a suggestion.

FIRST LORD: That's not how this works.

WILLIAMSON: Want to hear my suggestion?

FIRST LORD: No?

WILLIAMSON:

FIRST LORD:

WILLIAMSON: Okay, cool. Here it is. So, we need to call this sub something *cool*, right? Something *inspiring*.

FIRST LORD: I—

WILLIAMSON: Stay with me. Something *heroic*.

FIRST LORD: Minister...

WILLIAMSON: Here it is: HMS *Rogal Dorn*.

FIRST LORD: HMS *Royal Dawn*?

WILLIAMSON: *Dude*. No! Rogal Dorn. Oh man, how do
                you *not* know about Rogal Dorn?! Rogal
                Dorn is a hero of the Imperium.

FIRST LORD: The Royal Navy is proud of its
                history, but to many the empire is—

WILLIAMSON: No! Not empire! The Imperium of Man.

FIRST LORD:

WILLIAMSON: From *Warhammer 40K*.[*]

FIRST LORD:

WILLIAMSON: That's why this works, dude.
                It's inclusive. Everyone loves
                Warhammer 40K.

FIRST LORD: You want to name our new submarine
                after a science-fiction character?

WILLIAMSON: It's not science fiction. It's
                Warhammer 40K.

FIRST LORD: Aren't they the same thing?

WILLIAMSON: First Lord, you're just trolling me
                now, right?

FIRST LORD: I honestly don't know, sir.

WILLIAMSON: Anyway, I'm not talking about just
                any character. I'm talking about Rogal
                Dorn. The greatest of the Primarchs.
                He's a hero!

FIRST LORD: He's fictional.

WILLIAMSON: Oh, come on. We name ships after
                fictional people all the time, like
                Admiral Nelson.

---

[*] The painting of small figurines seems to have been a particularly common hobby for our
ancestors. Many of these figurines were made of lead. In *Ultragavine: An Illustrated History of
Gavin Williamson*, Dr Paul von Tillotson argues that this explains a lot about Williamson.

FIRST LORD: Wait, what? You think Horatio Nelson
               was fictional?

WILLIAMSON: One hand and one eye. The parrot.
               C'mon, dude.

FIRST LORD: What parrot?!

WILLIAMSON: The peg leg. Jim Hawkins.

FIRST LORD: That's Long John Silver!

WILLIAMSON: Aren't they the same?

FIRST LORD: No!

WILLIAMSON: Huh. Anyway, I still think HMS Rogal
               Dorn would be amazing.

FIRST LORD: I don't.

WILLIAMSON: Ideally, I'd go with HMS *Roboute
               Guilliman*, because my custom Space
               Marine Chapter is spun off from
               the Ultramarines. But Dorn was more
               badass, and the Fists are cool too.

FIRST LORD: Sir! It *cannot* be HMS *Rogal Dorn*!

[Downing Street. A little later]

LIDINGTON: What do you want, Gavin? You don't
               have an appointment.

WILLIAMSON: I need to speak to the prime minister.
               The navy are being stubborn.

LIDINGTON: [Laughing] Why, are you trying to
               name a submarine after a *Warhammer*
               character or something?

WILLIAMSON:

LIDINGTON: Oh God. You are.

WILLIAMSON: Rogal Dorn, dude!

WILLIAMSON: C'mon man. I just need five minutes.
                I want the prime minister to
                overrule them.

LIDINGTON: Gavin, fun as this would be to watch,
                I really can't let you go in there.

WILLIAMSON: Why?

LIDINGTON: Phil's in there.

WILLIAMSON: Oh.

[The prime minister's office. The same time]

MAY: Phil, the only thing I asked you for
                was a Brexit economic forecast.

HAMMOND: Which I did.

MAY: This is a sheet of A4 with 'We're
                FUCKED' scrawled on it. Not exactly
                comprehensive, is it?

HAMMOND: Oh sorry. Give it here... How
                about now?

MAY: You've just underlined the word
                'FUCKED' twice.

HAMMOND: Yup.

MAY: I can't publish this forecast.

HAMMOND: Why not?

MAY: Because, to risk repeating myself,
                it's a piece of paper with 'We're
                FUCKED' on it!

HAMMOND: As you can see, the fucked is now—

MAY: Yes, it is now underlined. I
                can see that.

HAMMOND: Twice.

MAY: Can't you at least add some
                optimism bias?

HAMMOND:	Oh, sure. Give it here... there you go.
MAY:	'We're FUCKED. LOL.'
HAMMOND:	That optimistic enough for you?
MAY:	It can't be that bad, surely?
HAMMOND:	Oh really? Would you like a second opinion? Can I borrow your phone...
MAY:	What are you—
HAMMOND:	Mark! It's Phil. How are things at the Bank of England? Yeah, we'll be online later, sure! Anyway, listen, I need a favour. I'm going through the economic forecast with the prime minister and... brilliant. Hang on. I'll put you on speaker.
MARK CARNEY:	[On speakerphone] Can y'all hear me now, Prime Minister?
MAY:	Hello Mark.
CARNEY:	Theresa, we are *fuuuuuucked*...
HAMMOND:	Thanks for that, Mark.
CARNEY:	No problemo, Phil. See you online in a bit, buddy.

MAY:	Frictionless trade can't be that important, surely?
HAMMOND:	Oh sure. It's not like Europe came together post-war and created some kind of overarching 'union' to facilitate it or something.
MAY:	Phil. I'm trying to present a positive outlook for post-Brexit Britain and I have to say, you're being spectacularly unhelpful here.
HAMMOND:	Oh, you noticed?

MAY: Why are you being so obtuse?

HAMMOND:

MAY: And why do you keep shadow-briefing
                the press that Brexit is bad for
                the economy?

HAMMOND:

MAY: Why do you... Phil! Say something!
                Stop pointing at the piece of paper
                that says 'We're FUCKED'!

HAMMOND: I mean, it answers all those
                questions.

MAY:

HAMMOND: Do you need anything else? It's just
                I promised Mark we'd play *Fortnite*...

MAY: No, it's fine, you can go.

HAMMOND: [Closing the door] Cheers.

MAY:

WILLIAMSON: [Opening the door] Prime Minister, I
                need you to approve—

MAY: Go away, Gavin, before I gut you with
                a teaspoon.

WILLIAMSON: [Quickly] Righto.

[The Ministry of Defence. Later that afternoon]

WILLIAMSON:

FIRST LORD: Do you need to look at the
                list again?

WILLIAMSON:

FIRST LORD: Minister?

WILLIAMSON:

FIRST LORD: Here you are, sir.

WILLIAMSON: Fine. This one.

FIRST LORD: HMS *Warspite*. A good choice sir. A
               proud history.

WILLIAMSON: [Muttering] It's no Rogal Dorn.

CHAPTER SEVEN

HAILING TO THE GRAYLING

In an attempt to shore up support for her deal, in the face of a potential Commons rebellion and negative economic forecasts, the prime minister began a whirlwind press tour of the regions and key allies.

```
[Somewhere in Scotland]

MAY:          Where are we today and who am I
              talking to?

LIDINGTON:    This is Scotland, and they're
              fishermen.

MAY:          Christ. We're Tories, David! Since
              when do we give a shit about the
              fishing industry? It's only good for
              two things: evacuating beaches and
              picking fights with Iceland.*

LIDINGTON:    They're pro-Brexit.

MAY:          Fuck's sake. It just makes no
              sense. We've been ignoring fishing
              communities for decades. Why would
              they back us now?

LIDINGTON:    Labour have been ignoring them too.

MAY:          Ah.
```

---

* The United Kingdom fought two wars with Iceland in the twentieth century over the subject of fishing rights. It seems these ended in draws.

LIDINGTON: The tragedy of desperation is that it brings false hope, to which we must now appeal.

MAY: Well, that's depressing. Shakespearean, but depressing.

LIDINGTON: Brexit means Brexit.

MAY: Did this venue at least get my rider?

LIDINGTON: Yes. Here. A bowl of M&M's with all the red ones picked out.

MAY: Thanks. Who's in charge back home, by the way?

LIDINGTON:

MAY: David...

LIDINGTON: Look, it had to be someone who couldn't hurt us...

MAY: Oh no.

[Downing Street. The same time]

GRAYLING: This is a bloody big office.

GRAYLING: [Spinning in his chair] *Wheeee!* Okay. David left a list of things to do. I should... Oooh! A box with buttons!

BOX WITH BUTTONS: Yes, sir?

GRAYLING: Blimey! There's a tiny man in it! Do you need help, little man in the box?

INTERCOM: This is the intercom, sir.

GRAYLING: Do you need help, little man in the intercom?

[In Scotland]

MAY: You put *Chris Grayling* in charge?!

LIDINGTON: What was I meant to do?! Literally
                everyone in the Cabinet is plotting
                against you.[*]

MAY: So is Chris!

LIDINGTON: Yes. But he's *useless* at it.

MAY: And now he's in charge of the country!

LIDINGTON: Look, it's just a week. What could
                possibly go wrong?

[The Kremlin. The same time]

AIDE: Chris Grayling is in charge.

VLADIMIR   Invade Ukraine.
PUTIN:

[Downing Street]

MAY: What about Stephen?

LIDINGTON: He's not told his family that he's
                Brexit Secretary yet. He's still
                working up the courage. I didn't want
                to out him.

MAY: Phil?

LIDINGTON: He's up here with us. I could ask
                Michael, but you said—

MAY: No. Not Gove. He's busy.

---

[*] 'The May government represents the only time in UK political history where it was quicker
to count the MPs not plotting against the prime minister, rather than those who were.'
Melanie Jackson, *An Absolute State: A History of England From Brexit to Boris*

LIDINGTON: I know, but do you *really* think
                he can persuade MPs to vote for
                your deal?

MAY: He's an eldritch fucking horror,
                David. He has ways and means.

─────────────────────

[Down south. A little later]

SAM GYIMAH: [Opening the door] Yes? Hello?
                Who— *aargh!*

GOVE: <Lich howl>

GYIMAH: Jesus *Christ*, Michael.

GOVE: gaH. sOrRY. ThE SkIN SuIT SLiPPeD.

GYIMAH: It's fine. I'm fine. Just give
                me a second.

GOVE: sORry. AnYWay, WOuLD yOU vOTe wiTH
                ThE Pm? I bRInG yOU a BOx oF PuPPIes
                aS aN OFFerINg.

GYIMAH: Oh. Thanks, that's... *Christ!*
                They're all dead!

GOVE: FuCK! AiRHoLEs. StuPID MicHAEL!
                FleSHLiNGs nEEd aIR.

─────────────────────

[Another house. Later again]

CHOPE: And that's why...

GOVE: CaN I jUST SaY that I aM suCH a fAN?

CHOPE: Sorry?

GOVE: bLOCkinG tHE upSKirT anD FGM BiLLs
                oN pROceDURaL teCHNIcALiTIEs? I'm
                aN UnDEad HoRROr fROm tHe DeMON
                diMEnsIONs anD tHaT sEEmEd SHiTTy
                eVEn tO mE.

CHOPE:	Look, not *all* men...
GOVE:	SqUEee! I aM fANboYIng sO hARd riGHT nOW!

[And another. Still later]

KAREN BRADLEY:	Michael, I hear what you're saying, but I'm the Northern Ireland Secretary.
GOVE:	sO?
BRADLEY:	This deal creates a border between Ireland and the mainland. If I back it, then how can I look the Northern Irish in the eye?
GOVE:	iF yOU DoN'T baCK iT, i MaY rIP theM OuT.
BRADLEY:	What?!
GOVE:	NoTHiNG.
BRADLEY:	Micheal, what is happening to your face?
GOVE:	i'M aTTEmpTING a diSArmING smILE.
BRADLEY:	It's... it's not working.

[A hotel bar in Scotland. That evening]

MAY:	Whiskey. Large. Oh, hello Phil.
HAMMOND:	Prime Minister. So how were the Scottish fishermen?
MAY:	A little bit racist.
HAMMOND:	Ah. Just as you like 'em.
MAY:	I'm not a racist, you know.
HAMMOND:	Oh sure. You just hate immigrants.

MAY: I don't!

HAMMOND: Stuck 'Go Home' on the side of any
            white vans lately?

MAY: I wasn't consulted about that.

HAMMOND: And how's that 'hostile environment'
            going? They still love that over at
            the Home Office, I hear.

MAY: Remind me why I'm stuck up here with
            you again?

HAMMOND: Lidington's rushed back to deal with
            Grayling and the Ukraine situation,
            and someone had to stay here and talk
            to the Scottish National Party MPs.

MAY: My joy is unconfined. Is that why
            there's a half-empty bottle of whiskey
            in front of you?

HAMMOND: The booze? Oh no. This is your fault.
            You asked Barnier[*] for an amended
            deal, didn't you?

MAY: Yes. How did you know?

HAMMOND: I picked it up from reception on the
            way through.

MAY: Thanks. Give it here. I don't... Wait
            — that absolute *fucker*.

HAMMOND: At least I *think* it's the same deal.
            It's just now written in Emoji. So I
            can't tell.

MAY: That man is not as funny as he
            thinks he is.

HAMMOND: I've got Ken Clarke working on a
            translation.

---

[*] French politician Michel Barnier was appointed by the EU to lead Brexit negotiations in 2019. His son and grandson would later hold the same role.

HAMMOND:	How's Gove been getting on down south?
MAY:	I've not had a chance to ask. Actually, wait. Bartender! Can you turn that TV up?
LAURA KUENSSBERG:	[On BBC News] Is it true that you plan to vote for the prime minister's deal, and are encouraging other MPs to the same?
GOVE:	[On TV] ThE Pm HaS mY fULL suPPOrt, oBViouSLY. BuT iF sHE is WatCHINg, I nOTe tHAT *SuNLESs SkIEs* iS OuT soON oN SteAM.
MAY:	That little fucker.
HAMMOND:	Nice choice. Should be a good game. At least it sounds like he's made some progress with MPs.
MAY:	God, I hope so.
KUENSSBERG:	[On TV] Is it true that you gave Sam Gyimah a box of dead puppies earlier today?
MAY:	Wait, *what?*
GOVE:	[On TV] ThEY weRe ALiVe unTIL hE OpENed ThE bOX.
MAY:	Bartender! Another whiskey!
HAMMOND:	[To the bartender] Maybe just leave us the bottle, again.

[The hotel bar in Scotland. Later that night]

MAY:	Look, I can get this through Parliament. We've been through this.
HAMMOND:	How? You'll have to get it out of Emoji, for a start. And then what? What's the point of any of this?

MAY: Brexit means Brexit.

HAMMOND: That's not a proper answer.

MAY: Neither was 'We're FUCKED'.

HAMMOND: Touché.

[Later still]

HAMMOND: [Slurring] Look, the point I'm
                making is this deal isn't...
                well... *anything*.

MAY: It's a compromise.

HAMMOND: There *is* no compromise. There never
                was. Let's call a spade a spade here.
                The hard Brexiteers in this Cabinet
                are idiots. The rest of us are
                fucking idiots too. Just pick a side.
                Fire them. Or fire me. *Fuck*. Make a
                decision. *Lead*.

MAY: Leading means finding a third way.

HAMMOND: No. Sometimes leading just means
                admitting that there *is* no third way.
                Rees-Mogg is a moron. Boris is a
                sociopath. I'm an egotist. But do you
                know one thing we *all* have in common?
                We know that there *isn't* a third
                way. This isn't going to end with a
                compromise. You're the prime minister.
                Pick a side.

MAY: Phil, I think you're drunk.

HAMMOND: I think I'm not drunk enough. Sod it.
                I'm going to bed.

CHAPTER EIGHT

A MAN OF FEW WORDS

In December 2018, a key question for many Brexiteers was whether the 'backstop' that the prime minister's deal contained would lock Britain into a customs union with the EU. With rumours swirling that a letter to the Cabinet from Attorney General Geoffrey Cox had confirmed this, MPs in the House of Commons demanded its publication.

———————

[Parliament. John McDonnell's office]

JOHN McDONNELL:[*]   Okay, Keir, you're Shadow Brexit Secretary, so walk me through today.

KEIR STARMER: Right, well, *in theory* the Attorney General will stand up, announce he is publishing his legal advice on Brexit, calmly sit down and we all leave happy.

McDONNELL: Geoffrey Cox?

STARMER: Yup.

McDONNELL: A man the Sheriff of Nottingham[†] would tell to calm down a bit?

STARMER: Yup.

McDONNELL: That's not going to happen, then.

---

[*]   Shadow Chancellor of the Exchequer from 2015 to 2019.
[†]   'Greedy, overly dramatic, self-serving rulers have long been a tradition in British mythology. This is one of the reasons why scholars assumed for some time that Lord Johnson was fictional.' M. F. McAndrew, *Myths and Legends of the Beforetimes*

STARMER: Nope.

McDONNELL: So, assuming he refuses to publish it—

STARMER: And he will refuse.

McDONNELL: ... Right, then what next?

STARMER: Ah. Well, that's when things get
              really interesting and awkward for the
              government. You see we'll—

McDONNELL: Yes?

STARMER: ... write him a letter!

McDONNELL:

STARMER:

MCDONNEL: That's it? Sorry, I was assuming you
              were going to say more than that.

STARMER: Oh, it'll be a strongly worded
              letter, trust me.

McDONNELL: Well, thank God for that.

STARMER: I don't think you realise how serious
              this letter is.

McDONNELL: Well, clearly.

STARMER: It will officially put him in
              contempt of Parliament!* That's
              serious business, with actual
              punishment attached.

McDONNELL: Okay, now we're talking. Tell me more.
              What's the punishment?

STARMER: He'll have to pay a small fine.

McDONNELL:

STARMER: I know, right!

---

*   'Until 2019, being held in contempt of Parliament was seen as a major transgression. After
    2019, it became a requirement for holding senior office.' Alys Kowalik, *(Un)Common Sense:
    The Rise and Fall of British Parliamentarianism*

McDONNELL: So let me get this straight. Our plan
is to embarrass Geoffrey Cox and the
prime minister, two people who have
shown no tendency to give any actual
fucks about parliamentary tradition
at all, through the threat of a
small fine?

STARMER: Yes.

McDONNELL: It's a shit plan, Keir.

STARMER: Do you have a better one?

McDONNELL: Okay, fair point.

McDONNELL: Fine. Write the letter then.

STARMER: Well... there's actually a bit
I left out.

McDONNELL: What?

STARMER: You're not going to like it.

McDONNELL: Keir...

STARMER: We'll need more than just Labour
signatures on the letter, so...

McDONNELL: You need me to talk to the Scots,
don't you?

STARMER: Yeah. I'll handle the rest.

McDONNELL: Oh, for fuck's sake...

[The House of Commons. A little later]

McDONNELL: Here. Done. The SNP are in.

STARMER: Perfect! I got the Greens, Liberals
and the Democratic Unionists to
sign up, too.

McDONNELL: You got the DUP to sign? How?!

STARMER: It's probably best not to ask.

_____

[The DUP offices. Earlier]

STARMER: Sign here, please.

NIGEL DODDS: Okay... Wait, what is this?

STARMER: Um, it's... a renewable energy rebate?

DODDS: Oh, right, no worries.

_____

[The Commons, again]

McDONNELL: Cunning.

STARMER: Well, I figured they'd got form.

McDONNELL: Brilliant. So we're all set, then.
                What happens now?

STARMER: Now is the easy bit. It just needs
                to clear the Standards Committee, but
                that shouldn't be a problem. There
                are always three Labour MPs sitting
                on that, so—

McDONNELL: Shit!

STARMER: What?

_____

[The Commons. A month earlier]

McDONNELL: We need to nominate someone new for
                Standards. Jess Phillips is down for
                it. Do we like her?

JEREMY   <Wry grin>
CORBYN:

McDONNELL: Righto, I'll block the appointment.

STARMER: You blocked Jess Phillips for
             Standards?! She's one of ours!

McDONNELL: Look, it's not my fault! Jez told
             me to do it.

STARMER: He told you?

McDONNELL: Well, he smiled, wryly.

STARMER: That's not the same thing.

McDONNELL: He doesn't speak, Keir! You want to
             know how hard my job is? Last week I
             thought he was in favour of a second
             referendum. Started briefing the press
             and everything. Then it turned out he
             was just holding in a fart.

CHAPTER NINE

DOBBY INTERVENES

As 2018 drew to a close, the prime minister finally looked to bring her Brexit deal to a vote in Parliament. With questions being asked about whether she had the numbers to pull it off, everyone was looking for some kind of sign.

———————————

[Downing Street]

MAY: So how does the Brexit vote look?

LIDINGTON: Thirty votes.

MAY: Okay. That's not as bad as I thought.
            If we lose by that, I can survive.

LIDINGTON: No, that's how many votes we'd get.

MAY: Oh. *Oh.*

LIDINGTON: Yes. Sorry. Wait... it's twenty-nine.
            I keep counting Grant Shapps twice.

———————————

[An allotment. The same time]

STARMER: Gentlemen, I've done the maths and
            the Tories are going to lose.

CORBYN: <Wise grin>

McDONNELL: Well, this is it. What do we do, Jez?
            Go for no-confidence? J. K. Rowling's

on Twitter saying we should call for a 'People's Vote'.[*]

CORBYN: [Scribbling]

STARMER: He's drawing! It's...

McDONNELL: It's a picture of Dobby the House Elf.[†]

STARMER: What does that mean?

McDONNELL: Thank you for your counsel, oh wise one.

CORBYN: <Serene look>

McDONNELL: We will ponder this and take action.

––––––––––––––––

[En route to Parliament. A little later]

STARMER: It's a picture of Dobby.

McDONNELL: I know what it is.

STARMER: What does it mean?

McDONNELL: Well, I don't fucking know, Keir. You know Jez. He's... what do you call it? In... in—

STARMER: Infuriating?

McDONNELL: Inscrutable.

STARMER: So, what are we meant to do, then? We don't have a plan.

McDONNELL: Wait. I've got an idea...

STARMER: What are you doing?

---

[*] One of the curious elements of the tapes is how strongly the opponents of Brexit seemed to believe that a population who had already demonstrated they were a little bit racist would suddenly change their minds.

[†] House elves were happy slaves who featured in popular children's fiction at the time. With hindsight, this is seen as explaining a lot about our ancestors.

McDONNELL:	I'm taking a photo of the Dobby picture.
STARMER:	Why?
McDONNELL:	Because we don't *have* to know what it means, Keir.
STARMER:	I still don't get it.
McDONNELL:	<Click> I'm simply going to email it to every fucker in Parliament and let Rorschach do the rest.

[A conference room. Five minutes later]

REES-MOGG:	And what I really want to know is why nobody talks about *men's* rights...
CHOPE:	Moggy, look!
REES-MOGG:	Dobby! You know what this means?
CHOPE:	Do tell!
REES-MOGG:	Dobby is a reminder that everyone should know their place. Send word to all! Letters must go in! The ERG are going to war!
CHOPE:	Huzzah!

[In Paris. *Simultanément*]

AIDE:	*Mon président! Regardez!*
MACRON:	*C'est Dobby!*
AIDE:	*Oui. Un Dobby magnifique.*
MACRON:	Dobby is a symbol of fraternity among all beings. I was wrong. Raise the minimum wage.
AIDE:	*En anglais?!*

74

MACRON: Oh, don't make such a big thing about
                 it, René. It was just easier.

———————————

[In Cabinet. The same time]

AMBER RUDD:[*]   Prime Minister, if we lose this
                 vote there'll be chaos. Markets will
                 tumble. Panic will reign.

GOVE: <Lich wail>

MAY: Michael says that isn't as bad as
                 it sounds.

RUDD: Of course he does! He's an
                 undead horror!

GOVE: <Sorrowful mewling>

RUDD: Sorry, Michael. 'Eldritch being.'

GOVE: <Happy gurgle>

———————————

RUDD: I'm just... wait. Did you all get
                 that email?

GRAYLING: Oh! What a *lovely* Dobby picture!

MAY: Is that by Jeremy?! *Shit.*

GRAYLING: The linework is glorious.

MAY: Dobby is a symbol of the oppressed
                 masses. Labour are about to act.
                 Hook the vote!

LIDINGTON: But Prime Minister...

MAY: *Do it now!*

———————————

[*] Amber Rudd held a number of positions during the key early years of Brexit, including
that of Home Secretary. Unfortunately her career as a Conservative MP was limited due to
occasional bouts of conscience.

[Somewhere grim. That night]

MAY: Where am I?

GOVE: YoU aRE aSLEep. I hAVe cOmE tO yoU In
                YoUR drEAms sO We mAY tALK.

MAY: Michael?! What is this place? It's so
                cold. So sad and grey. Like the soul
                of a dead clown.

GOVE: I hAVe broUGHt yoU iNTo mY
                ElDRitCH rEAlm.

MAY: It reminds me of Blackpool.[*]

GOVE: ReALLy? I'Ve NeVER beEn.

MAY: Anyway... speak, foul demon.

GOVE: BIt hARSh.

MAY: You've literally invaded my dreams
                with a vision of Blackpool.

GOVE: I kNow, bUt StILL...

MAY: Get to the point, Michael.

GOVE: wHEn yOU wAKe: reMEMBer. StEAm haVE a
                sALe oN. WOoOo.

MAY: What?

GOVE: jUSt ReMEmBER. WoOoo.

MAY: But why?

GOVE: WoOOo.

MAY: Yes, I got that bit.

—————————

MAY: [Snapping awake] Gah. Is that the
                phone? It's six a.m. Who's calling at
                this... hello?

[*] Blackpool would, of course, later suffer accidental atomic destruction due to Gavin Williamson's actions in the Moggist revolt. We thus think of it today as a radioactive wasteland. It is worth remembering that it wasn't always this nice.

76

LIDINGTON: It's me.

MAY: David?! Do you know what fucking time it is?!

LIDINGTON: Yes, but this is important. The ERG are moving against you again. Forty-eight letters of no confidence are in; they plan to call on you to resign.

MAY: What?! Wait... hang on... Michael... That little *fucker*!

LIDINGTON: Prime Minister?

MAY: David, get me Michael Gove's Steam wishlist again, and my credit card.

[Westminster. That afternoon]

MAY: Well, that Commons session was brutal.

LIDINGTON: Look, Theresa. I don't want to, but I do have to ask...

MAY: I'm not quitting, David.

LIDINGTON: But...

MAY: David, what's Chris up to right now?

LIDINGTON: Grayling? I gave him some Stickle Bricks to play with until nap time.

MAY: If I quit now, he's the next prime minister.

LIDINGTON: Sweet Jesus, you're not serious?!

MAY: I am. If I quit, then Grayling will likely become prime minister.

LIDINGTON: But he's an idiot!

MAY: Yes. But he's also not racist, corrupt, black, rabidly Remain, rabidly Brexit or Michael Gove. He's the human

77

	equivalent of a Twitter egg and that makes him least-worst candidate.
LIDINGTON:	Good God. Chris can't be prime minister.
MAY:	You watch. It'll be him or Boris.
LIDINGTON:	Johnson?! The man thinks he's Churchill.
MAY:	He's *a* Churchill. Just not the one he thinks he is. He's Randolph, the randy, syphilitic one that all the little old ladies love.
LIDINGTON:	What about Amber Rudd?
MAY:	Windrush scandal.
LIDINGTON:	Wasn't that your fault?
MAY:	Meh. Potatoes, *po-ta-toes*, David.
LIDINGTON:	Liam Fox for prime minister, then?
MAY:	Fox's 'controversies' section on Wikipedia has *actual subsections*. He's so creepy that even Gove avoids him.
LIDINGTON:	Gove, then!
MAY:	Eldritch horror, David.
LIDINGTON:	We've done it before.
MAY:	No, Michael Howard was a lich. Know your *Monster Guide*.
LIDINGTON:	Okay. Say Grayling does become prime minister by default...
GRAYLING:	<Schplop> Hello!
LIDINGTON:	Damnit! That was three times!
GRAYLING:	I made a Stickle Brick house. Do you like it?
MAY:	Very nice, Chris.

GRAYLING: And Gove says he's going to throw a
pizza party for me!

LIDINGTON: *Bloody hell.*

MAY: See what I mean?! That's why I'm not
quitting. Now, get me Gove's wishlist.

CHAPTER TEN

CAPEX VS OPEX

With talk of issues shipping goods across the Channel in a no-deal scenario, Secretary of State for Transport Chris Grayling decided to reassure the public that his department had everything in hand...

[A branch of Greggs near Parliament]

MAY: What? I'm in Greggs.*

LIDINGTON: [On the phone] Chris is on the radio.

MAY: It's fine. I told him to go on *Today*†
              and pretend we give a shit about rail
              fares going up.

LIDINGTON: Yeah... well... he's talking
              about Brexit.

MAY: Fuck.

LIDINGTON: Apparently, he's started some kind of
              shipping firm?

MAY: What?!

LIDINGTON: He's talking about how he's got a
              ferry company, or something?

MAY: Hook him off the air!

LIDINGTON: How?!

---

* 'It's notable how critical a role lukewarm sausage rolls played in the ritual history of our ancestors. Their consumption is assumed to have been a form of religious penance.' Janet Lovett, *The Piety of Pastry*

† The *Today* programme was a radio panel game. Government ministers were challenged to speak for one minute without hesitation, deviation or repetition on any subject other than on that which they'd been asked to comment.

MAY: I don't know! Call the studio or
                something?! Just do it!

                _____

[In Whitehall. Moments later]

HAMMOND: Well, what did she say?

LIDINGTON: That we need to get him off the air.

GRAYLING: [On the radio] So the people behind
                this are very clever. They don't
                own any ships, but they seem like
                lovely people and tell me that's not
                important.

HAMMOND: Should we use the curse?

LIDINGTON: Summon a minister while live on air?
                Are you mad?! The presenters would
                ask us serious questions about that!

HAMMOND: It's John Humphrys, David. He hasn't
                asked any serious questions since
                about 2005.

LIDINGTON: What do we do, then?

HAMMOND: Honestly? I think everyone is
                overreacting here. Chris talking
                utter shite isn't exactly front-page
                news any more.

GRAYLING: But don't think our freight planning
                is just limited to this new ferry
                company! We've really put some thought
                into this, John!

HAMMOND: Oh no. Hang on. He can't be about
                to... surely...

LIDINGTON: What?

HAMMOND: Don't do it, Chris!

GRAYLING: John, let me tell you all about this
                special thing I've got planned called
                Operation Dun—

HAMMOND:	Grayling! Grayling! Grayling!
GRAYLING:	<Schplop> —quack.

GRAYLING:	Oh. Hello!
LIDINGTON:	Why did you do that?! You said invoking him on air would be bad!
GRAYLING:	This is very confusing. I was on the radio... and now I am not.
HAMMOND:	Oh, come on! He was about to mention Operation Dunquack.
LIDINGTON:	What?
HAMMOND:	Dunquack!
MAY:	[Entering] What the fuck is going on? And what the fuck is Dunquack?
HAMMOND:	Wait... *neither* of you know?! Oh wow. Tell them, Chris!
GRAYLING:	Tell them what?
MAY:	What's Dunquack, Chris?
HAMMOND:	This is going to be so good...
GRAYLING:	Oh right! Well, we're going to disrupt the traditional shipping market.
MAY:	You what?
HAMMOND:	Here it comes...
GRAYLING:	By using lots of ducks.
MAY:	You *fucking* what?!

MAY:	You plan to ship freight.
GRAYLING:	Yes.
LIDINGTON:	Across the Channel.
GRAYLING:	Yes.

MAY: Using ducks.

GRAYLING: Yup. Operation Dunquack! Think of it
              as a sort of Duck Cloud.* Freight 2.0.

LIDINGTON: Oh my God. How many ducks?

HAMMOND: Forty-eight thousand. I had to sign
              the invoice.

GRAYLING: Well, only twelve thousand now, which
              I'm bloody annoyed about, because
              someone wouldn't pay for more food...

HAMMOND: That's because someone doesn't know
              his CapEx from his OpEx.

GRAYLING: You're starving my ducks!

MAY: Why are we still talking about ducks?

HAMMOND: You asked me to release the money
              to buy forty-eight thousand ducks.
              That's capital expenditure. You didn't
              ask for food money. That's operating
              expenditure.

GRAYLING: They're eating each other, Phil! And
              it's your fault! Do something about
              it! Or... or...

HAMMOND: Or what? What are you going to
              do? Send your mob of cannibal
              ducks after me?

GRAYLING: It's a 'raft', Phil. *A raft!* The
              collective noun for ducks is 'a raft'!

MAY: I should have stayed in bed today.

---

* An obsession with the power of clouds seems to have been a consistent theme among our
ancestors. This would come back to haunt them during the Second Dark Age, when many
companies and governments discovered that 'in the Cloud' just meant 'in someone else's
warehouse'.

83

GRAYLING: Prime Minister! Make Phil give me
               money for more ducks!

MAY: This is ridiculous. I don't even know
               where to begin with this...

HAMMOND: Why should I? Your other ducks will
               only eat them.

GRAYLING: I need to replenish the fleet!

HAMMOND: You mean the 'raft'.

GRAYLING: And I want money for duck food!

MAY: Oh my God, both of you shut up.
               I should never have let you plan
               the freight services, Chris. What
               was I doing?!

GRAYLING: [Sighing] Dunquack is a perfectly
               reasonable—

MAY: Shush. David, what are we going to do?

LIDINGTON: Same thing we always do in a crisis...

MAY: Blame Gordon Brown?

LIDINGTON: No. Outsource.

MAY: Who on earth is going to say that
               they can build a ferry service from
               scratch by March?

LIDINGTON:

MAY: David, no...

LIDINGTON: We have no choice.

MAY: Oh, for God's sake.

———————————

[Whitehall. Later]

LIDINGTON: Hello.

84

PACITA GUY:[*]   [On the phone] heLLO agAIN!

LIDINGTON: Look. We have another problem.
               We need...

PACITA GUY: iT'LL cOSt a HUnDreD mILliOn PoUnDS
               AnD bE rEAdy foR BreXIT!

LIDINGTON: Wait, I haven't told you what
               it is, yet.

PACITA GUY: GaH. SoRRY. I KeeP DoING tHaT, DoN't
               I? YoU FiRst. gO aHEad...

---

[*]   Again, the name of the company is weirdly hard to discern at this point in the tapes. It's almost like someone altered it for legal reasons.

CHAPTER ELEVEN

SPITFIRES SHOOTING LONGBOWS

As debate and confusion reigned in the Labour Party over whether to push for a general election or a second referendum, Home Secretary Sajid Javid decided to boost his leadership credentials by cracking down on immigration.

[A Corbyn rally. Backstage]

McDONNELL: What's he saying? I can't hear a word from back here.

STARMER: Something about General Electric,[*] I think.

McDONNELL: The old British defence contractor? Didn't they get broken up in the eighties?

STARMER: I think so.

McDONNELL: He's not *still* pissed about the Yarrow's Shipyard, is he? I've told him before that he needs to move on.

STARMER: *Sensible Brexit!*

McDONNELL: What?

STARMER: It wasn't 'General Electric'. It was something about 'a sensible Brexit'. That's what he's talking about.

---

[*] General Electric seem to have been a company that made both fighter jets *and* washing machines. However odd the Brexit era seems to us today, it is worth remembering that the 1970s seemed even stranger. Even to our ancestors.

McDONNELL: People don't want a sensible Brexit, Keir. They want one with Spitfires that shoot longbows at Frenchmen.

STARMER: Everyone is cheering now, though. Maybe he has a plan?

McDONNELL: They always cheer him, Keir. He could read out his shopping list and they'd all cheer. Then Owen Jones[*] would do an article about how it represents a breakthrough for everyday socialism.

STARMER: Now a woman at the front is touching him.

McDONNELL: That'll cure her scrofula.

STARMER: What is a 'sensible Brexit', anyway?

McDONNELL: I don't know, Keir. It's all bollocks.

STARMER: Maybe it's one where everyone queues nicely for their bread ration.

McDONNELL: The Scots can have independence, but only if they do it between nine a.m. and five p.m., Monday to Saturday.

STARMER: One where immigrants will be allowed in, as long as they're wearing business casual.

McDONNELL: To be fair, that would still make more sense than Sajid Javid's immigration proposals.

[Whitehall. The same time]

JAVID: So, you're all probably wondering why the Saj called this meeting of the COBRA committee.

WILLIAMSON: Hail, COBRA!

[*] Historians have been trying to explain the existence of Owen Jones for centuries, with little success. For the latest theories, see Professor John Hennigan, 'The Boy Who Would Be King' in *The English Journal of Owen Jones Studies*.

JAVID: Don't do that please, Gavin.
                We agreed.

WILLIAMSON: Sorry, Sajid.

JAVID: COBRA Commander. Call me COBRA
                Commander.

WILLIAMSON: Wait, you get to be COBRA Commander,
                but I don't get to say, 'Hail,
                COBRA'? That feels very unfair.

CHIEF   Do you actually need me here?
CONSTABLE
OF POLICE:

JAVID: Right. Well, as you all know the Saj
                has determined that we have an illegal
                immigration crisis on our hands.
                Chief Constable, you'll be our Gold
                Commander for this worrying situation.

CHIEF   Yes, sir. What's the scale of
CONSTABLE: the problem?

JAVID: Nine.

CHIEF   Blimey! Nine hundred illegal
CONSTABLE: immigrants? I can see the concern.

JAVID: No, nine.

CHIEF
CONSTABLE:

JAVID:

CHIEF   Are you worried they can't field a
CONSTABLE: full football eleven?

JAVID: I think we can all agree that this is
                an immigration crisis of unparalleled
                proportions.

CHIEF   Is it, though?
CONSTABLE:

WILLIAMSON:	Totally agree with you Sa— I mean, COBRA Commander.
JAVID:	Tough action is called for!
CHIEF CONSTABLE:	Sorry, but are we still talking about nine people?
JAVID:	Well, to start with. Indeed, checking online there are rumours circulating that another four have turned up.
CHIEF CONSTABLE:	Well, at least they have the beginnings of a substitutes bench now.
JAVID:	Look, this is a threat to our national security.
CHIEF CONSTABLE:	Thirteen desperate people in a couple of dinghies?
JAVID:	They're landing close to Folkestone! There's a nuclear power station nearby!
CHIEF CONSTABLE:	And also a really nice miniature railway. You think they're after that too?
JAVID:	Oh no! The Saj hadn't considered this...
CHIEF CONSTABLE:	I was *joking*.
JAVID:	Look, Chief Constable. You must see that—
FIRST LORD:	[Entering] Right. Who slid this meeting into my Outlook calendar without asking? Oh God.
WILLIAMSON:	Good to see you again, Admiral!
FIRST LORD:	I'm not an admiral.
WILLIAMSON:	Chaps, this is my top navy guy, summoned as requested.
JAVID:	Brilliant. Thanks, Gavin.

WILLIAMSON: No problem, COBRA Commander!

CHIEF
CONSTABLE: You lot activated the navy?!

FIRST LORD: I realise that I'm going to regret
asking this, but what's going on here?

JAVID: Imminent threat to the nation,
First Lord.

WILLIAMSON: Time for the Royal Navy to save the
country, once again.

CHIEF
CONSTABLE: Thirteen refugees in a dinghy.

JAVID: Two dinghies.

FIRST LORD: Two dinghies of refugees.

WILLIAMSON: Well, there may be more. And who
knows what nefarious weapons they're
packing. Do we still have battleships?
I've not been on a battleship yet!
Can we send a battleship?

FIRST LORD: This is the 'imminent threat'?

JAVID: Well, they *are* approaching Folkestone.

FIRST LORD: Have you been to Folkestone lately?
With respect, Minister, I think
that's more of an imminent threat to
the refugees rather than the other
way round.

CHIEF
CONSTABLE: Can we please show some sense
of perspective here? It's just
thirteen refugees.

JAVID: The Saj thinks you mean 'illegal
immigrants'.

CHIEF
CONSTABLE: No, I don't.

WILLIAMSON: Well, it's the same thing.

CHIEF CONSTABLE:	International law and basic human decency would beg to differ.
JAVID:	Yeah, well neither of those things vote in Tory leadership elections, do they?
FIRST LORD:	With respect, sir, the chief constable is right.
JAVID:	Oh great, so now *you're* an expert on the subject too?
FIRST LORD:	Home Secretary, the Royal Navy has been fishing desperate people out of the sea since the anti-slavery patrols of 1807. We know a refugee when we see one.
WILLIAMSON:	Everyone is a bloody critic.
FIRST LORD:	And on that note, I believe the navy's intervention here is not required. Goodbye, gentlemen.
CHIEF CONSTABLE:	That goes for me too.
JAVID:	Wait! You can't just...
[Door slams]	
WILLIAMSON:	Do I still have to call you COBRA Commander now?
JAVID:	Shut up, Gavin.

WILLIAMSON:	Sorry, Sajid.
JAVID:	That didn't really go how the Saj wanted.
WILLIAMSON:	I thought the navy would be a bit more up for it.
JAVID:	It's fine. The Saj is just a bit sad.

WILLIAMSON: Look, we could slap 'GO HOME!' on a
                van and drive around Hastings for a
                bit? The blue-rinse brigade love that.

JAVID: Meh. It's been done.

WILLIAMSON: Okay, well, how about we pop down to
                Dover quickly and do a photo call in
                front of the White Cliffs?[*]

JAVID: Not sure the Saj's heart is
                in it now.

WILLIAMSON: C'mon buddy... we can do stern faces
                as well! And point at the sea...

JAVID: Oh, go on, then.

[A Corbyn rally. Some hours later]

McDONNELL: Okay, here we go. KFC Megabucket.

STARMER: Oh, thank God. Why is it in
                a Leon bag?

McDONNELL: You think I was going to walk through
                that crowd with a KFC bag? I'd get
                lynched! Did I miss anything?

STARMER: Not really. Just that we need to show
                the 'kinder face of socialism'.

McDONNELL: [Munching] Kinder than what? The
                Tories are going to claim we're
                Stalinists whatever we do.

McDONNELL: Anything else?

STARMER: I don't think so. It's hard to tell
                after a while. Why isn't he like
                this with us?

McDONNELL: What do you mean?

---

[*] 'Challenging for the leadership of the Conservative Party required participation in a number of rituals. The most curious of these seems to have been standing at Dover while squinting worriedly at Calais.' Lisa Ashton-Riemers, *I'm Not A Racist But: Ritual Belief and Practice in the Conservative Party (1979–2029)*

STARMER: Well, he never bloody says anything,
              does he? He just makes faces and
              draws pictures. Yet out here in public
              he can waffle on for four hours about
              socialism and allotments.

McDONNELL: It's because they cheer for
              him. We don't.

STARMER: I'd happily cheer him if he gave me a
              definitive Brexit policy.

STARMER: Shit! Did you hear that?

McDONNELL: What? Sorry, I wasn't listening. I
              dropped a hot wing.

STARMER: He meant general election when he
              talked about 'consulting the people'
              in the press the other day!

McDONNELL: Is that bad?

STARMER: Yes! I thought he meant a second
              referendum. I've been hinting at that
              in the Chamber ever since.

McDONNELL: Didn't you ask him for guidance?

STARMER: Of course I did! But you know
              what he's like. He just smiled and
              gave me this.

McDONNELL: That's nice, that.

STARMER: It's a pencil sketch of D.Va from
              Overwatch.

McDONNELL: The shading on it is excellent.

STARMER: Would we actually win an election?

McDONNELL: Not according to the polls.

STARMER: Would the Tories?

McDONNELL: Depends. If it was May in charge,
              then it's a hung parliament again.
              Someone like Boris, we get smashed.

STARMER: So what's the point of calling for
              one, then?

McDONNELL: God knows.

STARMER: I mean, I like seeing Lord Buckethead[*]
              on TV as much as the next man, but
              once every five years is enough.

STARMER: Now he's talking about triggering a
              no-confidence vote.

McDONNELL: We won't win that either.

STARMER: I just don't get this. We're calling
              for an election we won't win via a
              no-confidence vote we won't win? I
              don't understand.

McDONNELL: Listen to the cheers though, Keir.
              And hey, look! That woman's scrofula
              has finally gone.

STARMER: It has?!

McDONNELL: Nope. But she thinks it has. Like
              everyone else in this place, that's
              good enough for her.

---

[*] Lord Buckethead seems to have been a curious member of the pre-crisis British aristocracy. A number of historians have attempted to chart the life of this strange figure, but sources are frustratingly limited. In *The Man in the Plastic Mask*, T. C. F. Gordon provides strong evidence that Lord Buckethead is the same person as Count Binface. Binface would die leading the decisive charge that broke the Moggist forces at the Battle of Clapham Common.

CHAPTER TWELVE

BORIS JOHNSON'S WEIRD SEX BUS

In an effort to boost flagging public opinion in her government, the prime minister attempted to bolster her NHS credentials with a number of empty policy announcements. Meanwhile, as negotiations on single-market access stalled, Chris Grayling staged a test run of the lorry queue system for Dover.

[A hospital in the north of England]

MAY: ... And so I'm *delighted* today to be announcing our NHS mental health plan in this new, state-of-the-art facility.

POLITICAL ADVISOR: Does anyone have any questions for the prime minister?

REPORTER: What do you say to suggestions this entire health plan is unfunded?

MAY: Well, I... that's a good question, but I'll leave that to the Chancellor here to... Phil..? David?!

[A traffic jam in Kent.[*] The same time]

HAMMOND: Where the *fuck* did all these lorries come from?

---

[*] It may seem weird now to think of Kent, centre of the Second Renaissance, as a place once dominated by concrete and traffic. But it was only after the French conquest that it flourished culturally. This was aided by the rise in sea levels that submerged Chatham.

STEPHEN: We're late! *Oh my God*. You said this
              would be a quick booze cruise!

LIDINGTON: She's going to kill us...

STEPHEN: It's eight in the morning. It's never
              busy at this time. Why is there a
              lorry jam?

LIDINGTON: Look, I'm driving; one of you at
              least try calling her. She's going
              to be livid.

HAMMOND: I've got no signal. Gah, how does
              anyone survive outside the M25?* It's
              awful out here.

STEPHEN: I'll try. I'm on the edge of signal.

HAMMOND: One bar?

STEPHEN: No, it says 'Edge'.

HAMMOND: That's not what it means, you idiot.

STEPHEN: Don't call me an idiot! I'm the
              Minister for Brexit!

HAMMOND: I'd say that proves my point—

LIDINGTON: *Just ring her!!*

STEPHEN: Shit. Too late, I've lost
              signal again.

LIDINGTON: Seriously, though, where did all these
              lorries come from?

HAMMOND: Check the satnav. Maybe we can take
              an alternative route.

LIDINGTON: I don't have one.

HAMMOND: What?!

LIDINGTON: This is a 1991 Volvo 240, Phil. It
              is a classic car. You *do not* put a
              satnav in a classic car.

---

* The moat that now surrounds and protects the New Hanseatic London follows the old route
of the M25 motorway.

HAMMOND:	Oh, for fuck's sake. Classic car? It's a fucking Volvo, David. From the period where they were available in any colour, as long as it was brown.
LIDINGTON:	I didn't hear you moaning about Cindy here back at Calais BeerMart.
HAMMOND:	Because it's a hatchback!
STEPHEN:	Wait, you named your car?
LIDINGTON:	Of course I did. Everybody names their cars, don't they?
STEPHEN:	I've never done it.
HAMMOND:	Actually, I'm with David here — it's not that unusual.
LIDINGTON:	Thank you, Phil.
HAMMOND:	Although most people don't give them a name that suggests they give sneaky handjobs behind King's Cross station.
LIDINGTON:	Phil!
HAMMOND:	Although this is a 1991 Volvo, so it does feel appropriate.
LIDINGTON:	Don't listen to him, Cindy, I think you're beautiful...
STEPHEN:	'... and please don't sell your story to the *Sunday Sport*.'
LIDINGTON:	Stephen!

[The hospital. Meanwhile]

REPORTER:	Prime Minister, will you answer the question? Is this NHS plan unfunded?[*]

---

[*] 'The decision to create the NHS was one of the few moments of sense and clarity shown by our ancestors in the twentieth century. One that they spent the next hundred years trying to undo.' Rebecca Edwards, *Carry on Doctor: Management in the NHS*

98

MAY: [Aside] Where in God's name are Phil
                  and David?! I don't do questions.

POLITICAL   We don't know.
ADVISOR:

REPORTER: Prime Minister?

MAY: [Aside] *Find. Them.*

REPORTER: Prime Minister! Can I get an
                  answer from you?

MAY: Um...

REPORTER:

MAY: Brexit means Brexit?

—————————————

[Kent. Where time means nothing]

STEPHEN: You could turn on the radio? Maybe
                  there'll be traffic news.

LIDINGTON: Okay. Although I think we can only
                  get medium wave...

ANNOUNCER: [On the radio] And next up, we have
                  Brexit Minister Kwasi Kwarteng.

HAMMOND: Hang on. I thought *you* were
                  Brexit Minister?

STEPHEN: I am! There's more than one of
                  us, you know.

HAMMOND: Really? Why?

STEPHEN: Because we're very busy.

HAMMOND: Doing what?!

STEPHEN: Important things. Making important
                  decisions.

—————————————

[Whitehall. The day before]

KWARTENG: Davis. Redwood. Boris.

STEPHEN: Avoid. Snog. Marry.

[The hospital. A short while later]

MAY: Well, that press conference was
              a disaster.

POLITICAL   Okay, well it's over now. Just the
ADVISOR: meet and greet.

MAY: Right. Shake babies, hold hands.

POLITICAL   Um, maybe the other way round?
ADVISOR:

MAY: Oh. Right. Sorry.

POLITICAL   Look, it's fine, ma'am. It's a
ADVISOR: hospital visit. It's low-key. Just
              talk to people. Be human.

MAY:

POLITICAL
ADVISOR:

MAY: I'm sorry. I thought you were about
              to explain how.

[Kent. Where time still means nothing]

HAMMOND: Do you think anyone voluntarily listens
              to local radio? This is terrible.

STEPHEN: Someone must do.

HAMMOND: If they do, they should probably be
              on some kind of watch list.

LIDINGTON: It's been forty minutes now and this
              lane is barely moving.

HAMMOND: The one next to us is moving fine.
              Just pull out.

LIDINGTON: No. It's bad road etiquette.

HAMMOND: You are such a Volvo driver.

LIDINGTON: I'll have you know that some of us
              see that as a compliment.

STEPHEN: I can't stop thinking about the prime
              minister. She must be getting so
              angry. This is terrible. *Oh Jesus*, I
              think I'm going to be sick...

LIDINGTON   [Together] Not in the car!!
/HAMMOND:

—————————————

STEPHEN: [Rolling the window back up] Okay. I
              feel a bit better now.

HAMMOND: Here, have a tissue.

LIDINGTON: Hang on. Someone is coming up on
              a scooter.

HAMMOND: And?

LIDINGTON: They've got a hi-vis jacket on. Maybe
              they know what's happen— oh no.

HAMMOND: What?

LIDINGTON: It can't be...

HAMMOND: David... What?!

GRAYLING: [Tapping the window] Hello!

—————————————

[The hospital. The same time]

MAY: How am I doing?

POLITICAL   Fine, it's just...
ADVISOR:

MAY:	What?
POLITICAL ADVISOR:	Maybe you could use the word 'fleshlings' less?
MAY:	But those babies were fleshy. I'm trying to be 'cute'.
POLITICAL ADVISOR:	It makes you sound like a Martian.
MAY:	What?!
POLITICAL ADVISOR:	Let's... let's just focus on talking to some adults.

———————————

[In Kent. An eternity unfolding]

GRAYLING:	Do you like my hi-vis jacket?
LIDINGTON:	What's going on, Chris?
GRAYLING:	Dunquack practice. Lorry section. We're out on manoeuvres!
HAMMOND:	Hang on, we're stuck in traffic because you're playing *Smokey and the Brexit*?
LIDINGTON:	Ha! Or *Total Con-voy*.
STEPHEN:	Hey! Brexit Minister! I'm right here!
HAMMOND:	I'm going to assume, from your mere presence in the area, that this traffic jam is your fucking fault.
LIDINGTON:	Now Phil, let's not jump to—
GRAYLING:	Oh yes. Totally. Sorry about that. I was testing our traffic-management plans.
HAMMOND:	And accidentally launched some kind of Kent Lorry Festival instead?

GRAYLING: To be honest, it's a fair description.
               Boris has turned up in a weird
               hippy sex bus.

[The hospital. The same time]

MAY: And how do you like being a nurse?

FEMALE NHS   I'm not a nurse.
WORKER:

MAY: Sorry! I meant a doctor!

FEMALE NHS   I'm a radiographer. Why do Tories
WORKER: always assume everyone in the NHS is
               a nurse or a doctor?

MAY: Look, I'm sorry, I'll just... oh,
               hello there. So how do you like being
               a nurse, or doctor, then?

SECOND FEMALE I'm a clinical biochemist.
WORKER:

MAY: Gah, you! How do you...

THIRD FEMALE   Biomedical scientist.
WORKER:

MAY: I'm confused. Is that the same?

BOTH: [Frostily] No.

MAY: Ooohkay... you! How do you like
               being a doctor?

MALE NHS   Bit sexist. I'm actually a nurse.
WORKER:

MAY: *Oh, come on...*

POLITICAL   Maybe we should just go.
ADVISOR:

[In Kent. The same time. Probably]

LIDINGTON: I'm still confused. What are you doing with these lorries?

GRAYLING: Cunning plan, you see?

HAMMOND: Oh, do tell.

GRAYLING: Scare the EU. I think they'll see how ready we are for Brexit and come back to the negotiating table!

LIDINGTON: Because you caused a big traffic jam?

HAMMOND: In our own country.

GRAYLING: Yup! It's brilliant, isn't it?

STEPHEN: It's... something.

HAMMOND: So exactly how big is this traffic jam?

GRAYLING: Well, I wanted to show how we'd handle the full stretch down to Dover. For that I needed about four thousand lorries.

LIDINGTON: You've got four thousand lorries here?!

GRAYLING: Oh God no. I wish. No, we managed to invite about a hundred and fifty.

HAMMOND: That's still a lot of lorries.

GRAYLING: Well, ah, no, actually. Only eighty-eight showed up. Plus Boris in his weird sex bus.

STEPHEN: Can we stop talking about that? I think I'm going to be sick again...

LIDINGTON/   [Together] Not in the car!!
HAMMOND:

LIDINGTON: So we're stuck on the A256 just so
                 you can prove a point?

GRAYLING: Wonderful, isn't it? Though you're not
                 really stuck.

HAMMOND: What?

GRAYLING: Well, you're only four lorries back
                 from the front and they're all in
                 this lane anyway. You could overtake.
                 That's why traffic's moving fine in
                 the other lane.

HAMMOND: I fucking told you, David! *Fucking
                 Volvo drivers!*

HAMMOND: Floor it, David!

LIDINGTON: I will *not* 'floor it'. Not only would
                 that be irresponsible, it would also
                 risk damaging the engine of this—

STEPHEN: *Can we please just go!*

GRAYLING: Oh, you aren't staying? You really
                 should hang around for the finale.
                 It's going to be *wonderful*. There are
                 some classic trucks here and we're
                 going to finish by doing some laps
                 round an old airport. Gives us a
                 chance to toot the big horns!

HAMMOND: I swear to God...

LIDINGTON: We're fine, Chris. Look, sorry, we've
                 got to go.

[Car drives off. Responsibly]

GRAYLING: [Sighing] Shame. Oh well.

<Clicks CB radio>

GRAYLING: Fluffy duckies, this is Papa Ducky. Form up and roll out. We got ourselves a convoy.

CHAPTER THIRTEEN

THE CHIMAY RED LINE

Having failed to get her deal through Parliament, Theresa May returned to Brussels in 2019 to try and get better terms from the EU, particularly with regards to trade across the Irish border. She left Phil Hammond in charge of the country. Allegedly...

———————

[In Brussels]

MAY: What's our plan for today?

LIDINGTON: More nationalistic flailing? It seems to be the only thing we've been good at so far.

MAY: Ha bloody ha. If I'd wanted sarcasm, I'd have brought Phil along.

LIDINGTON: Why didn't you?

HAMMOND: I had to leave someone sensible in charge back in the UK.

———————

[A queue of traffic just outside Calais. The same time]

STEPHEN: She's going to kill us. *Again*.

HAMMOND: Oh pipe down, Cameron Frye. Leave this
                to Ferris.[*]

STEPHEN: Why won't they let us through on to
                the ferry?

HAMMOND: I don't know. Stay with Chris and his
                stupid lorry. I'll go find out.

GRAYLING: Hello!

STEPHEN: Why did we bring this thing, anyway?

HAMMOND: Lidington wouldn't lend us the Volvo
                and Chris insisted on it.

GRAYLING: Always wanted to drive one of these.
                My CB tag is Papa Ducky!

[In Brussels]

MAY: Okay, thinking out loud: what if we
                dropped all import tariffs at the
                Irish border?

LIDINGTON: That sounds... bad.

MAY: Possibly, but let's at least run it
                past Phil.

[Outside Calais]

STEPHEN: She's going to find out.

HAMMOND: She's not. Don't think I haven't
                learned some lessons since last time.

STEPHEN: What if she calls the office?!

---

[*] 'Whenever someone claims our ancestors lacked our level of cultural sophistication, I point
them to *Ferris Bueller's Day Off,* a film in which your perception of who is the hero and who
is the villain depends entirely on the age of the viewer.' Hugh David, 'Searching for Shermer'
in *The Journal of Ancient Film and Cinema*

HAMMOND:	I activated my backstop.

[In Brussels]

MAY:	Phil!
RECORDING OF PHIL:	[On the phone] Yes, Prime Minister.
MAY:	So, David and I have been thinking. What if we—
RECORDING OF PHIL:	No, Prime Minister. It's a shit idea.

[Outside Calais]

STEPHEN:	Surely she'll notice it's a recording?
HAMMOND:	Never has before. I call it 'Robophil'.
STEPHEN:	How long have you used it?

[Flashback to April 2017]

MAY:	Phil!
ROBOPHIL:	[On the phone] Yes, Prime Minister.
MAY:	Should I call an election?
ROBOPHIL:	Yes, Prime Minister.

[Outside Calais. The present]

STEPHEN:	Well, that explains a lot.
HAMMOND:	I've got it set to say 'no' a lot more now.

[In Brussels]

LIDINGTON: What did Hammond say?

MAY: He swore and hung up.

LIDINGTON: That's 'no tariffs' off the table,
               then. Next?

MAY:

LIDINGTON:

MAY:

LIDINGTON: Don't say border drones again.

MAY:

LIDINGTON:

MAY: Dro—

LIDINGTON: Jesus *fucking* wept.

MAY: Don't swear, David. We've been
               through this before. You know it
               doesn't suit you.

MAY: Technology behind the border could...

LIDINGTON: We've been through this. It doesn't
               work and you still have to deal with
               smuggling!

MAY: Drones could—

LIDINGTON: Stop saying drones!

MAY: But they—

LIDINGTON: They'd what?! Fund public services
               through video sales to *Police, Camera,
               Action!*?!*

---

* 'The generation born immediately after World War Two seem to have spent most of their
lives watching old war films and police chases through Milton Keynes. With hindsight, it's
surprising the final collapse took as long as it did.' Mikaela Irish, *Boomtime: The Origins of
England's Great Collapse*

111

[Outside Calais]

HAMMOND: Okay. So they've finally told me why they won't let us in. It's because of Chris.

GRAYLING: Hello!

HAMMOND: He's banned from Calais, apparently.

STEPHEN: The Transport Secretary is banned from Calais? How does that even happen?

HAMMOND: I don't know, Stephen. But it's Chris, isn't it? So of course it does.

GRAYLING: Hello again!

STEPHEN: What are we going to do? Leave Chris behind?

HAMMOND: We can't. He's the one with the HGV licence.

STEPHEN: We could leave the lorry?

HAMMOND: Stephen, this may be the last Belgian booze run we can do in a while. I'm not leaving it here. Call this my Chimay red line.

[In Brussels]

MAY: We could threaten to walk away? Or call Barnier's bluff?

LIDINGTON: It won't work. The four freedoms[*] are more important to the EU than a short-term economic hit.

MAY: Let's run it past Phil anyway.

---

[*] Those studying the EU have long debated what the four 'freedoms of movement' were. Current scholarship leans towards: people, capital, services and Amazon parcels.

112

MAY: Phil!

ROBOPHIL: [On the phone] Yes, Prime Minister.

MAY: So, David and I have been thinking.
                  What if we—

ROBOPHIL: No, Prime Minister. It's a shit idea.

<Click>

MAY: He hates it.

[Outside Calais]

STEPHEN: Robophil won't fool her for ever.

HAMMOND: Don't worry, after two calls it
                  forwards to my mobile instead. Focus
                  on ideas. We need a plan to... what
                  are you doing?

STEPHEN: Calling Williamson. I'll put him
                  on speaker.

HAMMOND: Gavin? Why would you do that?! There
                  is no problem in life to which
                  the solution is Gavin Williamson.
                  Hang up! Hang—

WILLIAMSON: [On speakerphone] Primarch Gavinus
                  here! How may we serve?

HAMMOND: Oh, for fuck's sake. What does that
                  even mean?

[At the Ministry of Defence]

WILLIAMSON: Admiral!

FIRST LORD: We've *been* through this.

WILLIAMSON: Our brave boys have been trapped by
                the Frogs in Calais.[*]

FIRST LORD:

WILLIAMSON: Need you chaps to go and Dunkirk them.

FIRST LORD:

WILLIAMSON:

FIRST LORD: Minister?

WILLIAMSON: [Sighing] Hammond, Stephen and
                Grayling are stuck at Calais with a
                lorry full of booze. I need the navy
                to go and pick them up.

FIRST LORD: Sir...

WILLIAMSON: Look, think of it as a rehearsal
                for B-Day. Go and grab their lorry
                of supplies: bring it back.
                Simples.

FIRST LORD: Oh well, absolutely. Now you've put
                it that way. Shall I send one of the
                many, many roll-on/roll-off ferries
                to be found in the Royal Navy? Or
                just quickly fit HMS *Elizabeth* with a
                large crane?

WILLIAMSON: Is that sarcasm?

FIRST LORD: Sir.

WILLIAMSON: Was that... 'Yes sir'?

FIRST LORD: Sir.

[Outside Calais]

STEPHEN: Okay, Gavin says the navy won't help.

---

[*] 'Williamson, like many of his generation, looked down on the French for being unable to
accept their loss of world-power status. It was a handy way to avoid accepting their own
loss of world-power status.' James Cameron, *The Last Primarch: A Biography of England's
Worst General*

HAMMOND: *Quelle surprise.* Well, what if—
<Ringing> Shit! It's Theresa.
Keep quiet.

MAY: [On the phone] Phil! How about if
we... wait... why can I hear lorries?

HAMMOND:

GRAYLING: Hello!

MAY: And why is Chris with you?

HAMMOND: We're... playing *Eurotruck Simulator*
with Ken Clarke. *Callyoubackinabitbye!*

HAMMOND: I think she bought it for now, but
we have to get back to London. We
need a plan.

GRAYLING: I have a plan!

HAMMOND: To be a bit more specific, we need a
plan that will actually work.

GRAYLING: I could use the CB to find us a
driver, then you could summon me home
via the curse when you get back?

HAMMOND:

STEPHEN:

HAMMOND: Bloody hell.

STEPHEN: That's actually a really good
plan, Chris.

––––––––––

GRAYLING: Breaker, breaker. Papa Ducky stuck
on a backstroke at the chicken coop.
Need a pinch hit. Quack, my fluffy
ducklings!

VOICE FROM I can bat. Pos check?
THE CB:

GRAYLING: Calais. East side pickle park.

VOICE FROM THE CB:	Ten four.
HAMMOND:	What the fuck is happening?
STEPHEN:	I have no idea...

[Outside Calais. Twenty minutes later]

GRAYLING:	So this is Maciej.
MACIEJ:	Hello.
GRAYLING:	He'll drive the lorry back to London with you.
HAMMOND:	Honestly, this is good work, Chris.
STEPHEN:	We'll summon you back when we arrive.
GRAYLING:	Don't forget!
HAMMOND:	We won't. Seriously. Well done.

[Lorry drives off]

GRAYLING:	Goodbye chaps! Glad I helped!

[Outside Calais. Eight hours later]

LIDINGTON:	God, this ferry port is grim.
MAY:	We should have flown back.
LIDINGTON:	Cindy is cheap and very reliable.
MAY:	Please God, can you stop saying that, David. It sounds disgustingly grim. It's like having a conversation with Boris Johnson.
LIDINGTON:	Look at all these desperate people hoping to cross.
MAY:	Oh God, that one's coming over. David! Quick! Roll up the windows before—

116

GRAYLING: [Tapping the window] Hello!

MAY: Chris?!

GRAYLING: I think Hammond and Stephen have
              forgotten me.

MAY: Phil?! That lying snake! David, get
              us home. Now.

[Car drives off]

GRAYLING: Goodbye! Don't forget about me too!

CHAPTER FOURTEEN

THE TRAGEDY OF DUNQUACK

Debate continued in Parliament over the right way forward. Meanwhile, the consequences of bad financial planning became clear to Chris Grayling, with ominous consequences for all.

[Parliament. Outside Chris Grayling's office]

STEPHEN: Chris, I just wanted to stop by and apologise for leaving you in Calais. We... Chris? Are you okay?

GRAYLING: [Sobbing] She is all that remains of my beautiful little fleet.

STEPHEN: Oh! Huh. There's a duck in your office.

GRAYLING: She's the last survivor of Dunquack.

STEPHEN: Ooh-kay...

GRAYLING: I call her Margaret. They're all dead, Stephen. All forty-eight thousand of my fluffy little ducks. Except Margaret.

STEPHEN: How?!

GRAYLING: They started eating each other. It was horrible. I had no food for them!

STEPHEN: Why?

HAMMOND: [Passing by] Why do I have to keep explaining this? Because someone here doesn't know the difference between

118

                    capital expenditure and operational
                    expenditure.

GRAYLING: [Shouting] *You monster!*

HAMMOND: Nope. Me accountant.

STEPHEN: Chris! Come back! Don't run away!
                Damnit, Phil!

HAMMOND: What? What did I do?

STEPHEN: Don't be mean. Think about
                his feelings.

HAMMOND: Why? Think about mine. I just had to
                deal with 47,999 dead ducks.

STEPHEN: Yuck. Where are they?

HAMMOND: Well... let's just say London won't
                have a fried 'chicken' shortage
                post-Brexit.[*]

STEPHEN: So, what do we do now?

HAMMOND: About what?

STEPHEN: You know... Margaret.

HAMMOND: Who?

STEPHEN: The duck.

HAMMOND: Send out for some hoisin sauce?

STEPHEN: This isn't funny!

HAMMOND: Oh, come on. We're alone in Chris
                Grayling's office with a duck. It is
                kind of funny.

                    ———————————

HAMMOND: The last survivor of Dunquack, eh. I
                bet that duck's seen some horrors.

STEPHEN: Probably. I... no.

---

[*] Modern readers will note with some irony that it was indeed a lack of fried chicken that
     would eventually prompt London to revolt and found the New Hanseatic League.

HAMMOND:	What?
STEPHEN:	Look, this is silly. But... there's something weird about its eyes...
GOVE:	<Lich wail>
STEPHEN:	*Fucking hell!*
HAMMOND:	Your suit mic's off, Michael.
GOVE:	sORRy I sAID: 'thAt'S bECaUse iT iS nO LonGEr a DuCK.'
HAMMOND:	What are you doing here? It's Sunday. Shouldn't you be out rambling?[*]
GOVE:	yeS, I KnOW. tODay iS My DAy oFF.
HAMMOND:	And?
GOVE:	iN TruTH, i WAs dRAwn hERe bY aN EvENT rARE, gLOrIOUs aNd HoRRibLE. The BiRTh oF a nEW hORRor.
HAMMOND:	And that brought you to Chris Grayling's office?
GOVE:	WeLL, I trIED ChrISToPHeR ChOPeS's oFFIce FIrsT.
STEPHEN:	Naturally.
HAMMOND:	So, you're saying there's a *new* eldritch horror in the world?
GOVE:	YeS. iT Is rARe, bUT wHEN a BEiNG dOEs thINGs trULY hoRRIBle, caUSES PuRE suFFERing aND iS TrULY maLEvOLenT, iT CaN TransCEND moRTALitY aND bECoME a horROR.
STEPHEN:	And you're *sure* it's not Christopher Chope?
GOVE:	i CHeCKeD. TwICE.

---

[*] Walking through the countryside seems to have been a common hobby for our ancestors. Often accompanied by ceremonial littering, if the archaeological record is any guide.

HAMMOND: So you think Grayling's duck is an
            eldritch horror?

GOVE: YeS. bE WaRY oF iT. NoW I muST gO.
            FoR iT iS—

HAMMOND: Your day off. Yes, we know.

GOVE: GooDByE.

STEPHEN:

HAMMOND: Look, it's just a duck. He's being
            overly dramatic.

STEPHEN:

HAMMOND: Yeah. Of course. Let's go.

STEPHEN:

HAMMOND: Lock the door, though.

<Click>

M'GREH: qUAcK.

CHAPTER FIFTEEN

THAT'S NO DUCK...

The prime minister and Stephen headed back to Brussels to try and renegotiate the Brexit deal yet again. Meanwhile, a planned state visit to China by Phil Hammond was derailed after Gavin Williamson made ill-judged comments about their military capabilities in the press. With all this happening, the Cabinet met to find out how much progress had been made on post-Brexit trade deals.

[In Downing Street]

JAVID: Good morning, Prime Minister! The
                Saj is happy to... Oh. Phil. You're
                chairing. Shouldn't you be in China?

HAMMOND: Yes, but Gavin's been reading Biggles
                comics* again, and they've withdrawn
                my immigration visa to make a
                statement.

JAVID: Bugger. He doesn't learn.

HAMMOND: This time he fucking will.

[Gavin Williamson's office. The same time]

WILLIAMSON: [Crying] My Space Marines! Who broke
                all my Space Marines?!

---

*   Before they reached an age where watching war films and car crashes was acceptable, the Brexit generation grew up reading exaggerated tales about British soldiers fighting the fearsome 'Hun'. Again, a lot of the subsequent historical events make sense with hindsight.

[In Downing Street]

HAMMOND: Speaking of pointless posturing, how's your war on pregnant sixteen-year-olds going?[*] Stopped any more from coming home and ruining the country?

JAVID: Ha bloody ha. The Saj will not be seen to compromise on security!

HAMMOND:

JAVID: Anyway, she's nineteen now and has had the baby.

HAMMOND: Oh, that increases her threat level, certainly. Anyway. Let's get this meeting underway. As you've probably worked out, I'll be chairing today while... yes, Chris?

GRAYLING: Where's Theresa?

HAMMOND: In Brussels.

GRAYLING: And David?

HAMMOND: David is... busy.

[St Stephen's Tavern. The same time]

ANNA SOUBRY: It's just so nice being free from all the faction fighting.[†]

---

[*] During this period of history, successive Conservative governments were obsessively concerned about the militancy and threat potential of radicalised, pregnant teenage girls. Afghanistan would fall to the Taliban two years later. To our knowledge, no radicalised, pregnant teenage girls were involved.

[†] The Independent Group was a political party founded in 2019 by breakaway Labour and Conservative MPs such as Soubry and Greening. The Independent Group wanted to show there was an alternative to constant factionalism. It immediately succumbed to constant factionalism.

JUSTINE GREENING:	I can imagine.
SOUBRY:	Honestly, you should think about it. It feels... It feels...
GREENING:	Are you okay?
SOUBRY:	Yes. Sorry. It's just... that man over there. In the trench coat.
GREENING:	What about him?
SOUBRY:	He's watching us through two holes in a newspaper.
GREENING:	Oh, don't worry! That's just Lidington. He's my tail, apparently.
SOUBRY:	Your tail?
GREENING:	Yes. They're worried you'll persuade me to defect. So they're spying on me.
SOUBRY:	He's not very good at it.
GREENING:	I know.
SOUBRY:	Do you want me to go over there and have a word?
GREENING:	God, no. I've been putting all our drinks on his tab.

[The Cabinet. Meanwhile]

HAMMOND:	I've also got apologies here from Stephen. Apparently, he's in Brussels too. Talks on a possible Irish backstop with Barnier.
LIAM FOX:	Nice. How's that all going?

[In Brussels]

STEPHEN:

BARNIER:

STEPHEN: What about...

BARNIER: Nope.

STEPHEN:

BARNIER:

STEPHEN: Or...

BARNIER: Noooo.

[Cabinet]

HAMMOND: Oh, fucking swimmingly, I'm sure.
              Anyway, to business. Liam. Trade
              update please, can you—

MORDAUNT: Sorry, but is no one else going
              to mention that there is a duck
              in the room?

HAMMOND: Oh right. You missed that. It's...
              look... it's Chris Grayling's
              comfort duck.

MORDAUNT: Comfort duck?

GRAYLING: I call her Margaret.

M'GREH: qUAcK.

MORDAUNT: Comfort duck?

HAMMOND: [Sighing] Comfort duck. Just... go
              with it. Okay? Can we get back to—

GRAYLING: Would you like to stroke my
              quacker, Penny?

MORDAUNT: Oh wow. It's very soft.

HAMMOND:	Phrasing, people. *Phrasing*. Can we please think about how things will read in the minutes. In fact, how about everyone just forgets about the duck and...
M'GREH:	QUaCk
MORDAUNT:	Aw.
GOVE:	tHAt is nO dUcK. iT iS AN ELdrITCH hoRROr.
HAMMOND:	Oh *come. On*. Not this again.
JAVID:	It's just a duck, Michael.
M'GREH:	i WILL reNDeR yoUr PaRtY asUNDeR.
GOVE:	aHAh! sEE! DiD yOU heAR thAT?
FOX:	Yes. It quacked again!
GOVE:	nO iT DiDN't! It sAId...
M'GREH:	aLL WiLL bECoME chAOS.
GOVE:	ThErE! AgAIn!
MORDAUNT:	That's a cute quack.
GOVE:	HoW Are yOU NoT HeARinG ThIS?!
FOX:	Hearing what?
MORDAUNT:	Michael, are you all right?
M'GREH:	yOU wILL aLL PaY fOR yOur HUBris.
MORDAUNT:	It's so quacky!
GOVE:	iT iS nO DUcK!
M'GREH:	i wiLL CAsT yOU ALL DoWN INto a SEa oF etERNal FaRAgeS.
GOVE:	aWAy! I mUST pREPARE!

\<Flash of disappearing tentacles\>

HAMMOND:	Right. Well. *Anyway*.

HAMMOND:	Liam, are the forty trade deals you promised ready?
FOX:	We'll have up to forty deals in place, yes.
GRAYLING:	Brilliant! Go Team Brexit!
HAMMOND:	Sorry... 'up to'?
FOX:	Up to forty, yes.
HAMMOND:	See, there's that phrase again: 'Up to.'
FOX:	
HAMMOND:	How many, Liam?
FOX:	Okay, six.
HAMMOND:	Six?!
FOX:	Maybe... seven?
HAMMOND:	Who are the six trade deals with?
FOX:	Israel, the Palestinian Authority, the Faroe Islands, East and Southern Africa, and Chile.
MORDAUNT:	The Faroe Islands?!
FOX:	Yes. Look, they have a strong fishing industry.
MORDAUNT:	So do *we*!
HAMMOND:	That's not a trading bloc Liam. It's a car-boot sale.
FOX:	I think I can do a deal with the Swiss in time as well.
HAMMOND:	Well, *great*. Because I'd hate to pay tariffs on our chocolate and Nazi gold imports. For *fuck's sake*.
FOX:	There's no need to swear. I'm trying my best.

MORDAUNT: Have you got Japan, at least? That
              was the big one.

FOX: Yes.

MORDAUNT: Thank God.

FOX: By which I mean... no.

HAMMOND: Fuck. My. *Life*.

MORDAUNT: How do you not have Japan? That was
              so close when we all spoke last week!

FOX: Well yes, but they were dragging their
              feet. I got worried we were losing
              them, so...

[Jeremy Hunt's* office. The week before]

JEREMY HUNT: Hey! Good to see ya, pal. Why so sad,
              little fox cub?

FOX: I'm just a bit worried, Jeremy. Japan
              are taking ages to decide and...

HUNT: Gotta neg 'em, bro. Disrespect 'em.
              Make them think we don't need it.

FOX: I don't think...

HUNT: Give me a second. I think I've still
              got their details from... there. Done.
              Email sent. Thank me later!

HAMMOND: What the fuck did you do, Jeremy?

HUNT: Look, Phil, you know my philosophy.
              Always act the big man. In the NHS
              they used to refer to me as 'the
              biggest Hunt in any room'.

---

* Jeremy Hunt appears to have served in several key cabinet positions, including Secretary of State for Health and Chancellor of the Exchequer. There is some confusion over the spelling of his surname. Particularly in informal sources.

129

EVERYONE:

HUNT: What?

MORDAUNT: That's... not *quite* what they
               used to say.

HUNT: Really? What was it, then?

MORDAUNT: <Whispers>

HUNT: Well, that's just bloody *rude*.

HAMMOND: Pretty fucking accurate right
               now, though.

HAMMOND: Right. So, let's recap. The *one thing*
               we've done this week is make China and
               Japan reach an agreement on something.
               The first time that's happened since
               World War Two. And it's that *we're*
               idiots. Good work, everyone. God, I
               hope Theresa's day is going better.

[In Brussels. The same time]

MAY:

JUNCKER:

MAY: What about...

JUNCKER: Nope.

MAY:

JUNCKER:

MAY: Or...

JUNCKER: Noooo.

CHAPTER SIXTEEN

THE BREXIT CLUB

In an attempt to demonstrate her control over the party, the prime minister cracked down on a number of acts of minor rebellion in the early months of 2019. For a few in the Cabinet, this led to detention...

[Parliament. Saturday morning]

JULIAN SMITH: So, let's see. Who has Castle Mayskull sent me this morning... a princess, a geek, a basket case, a rebel and... a Grayling.

ESTHER McVEY:[*] Hey.

WILLIAMSON: What?

RUDD: [Sticking her tongue out]

HAMMOND: Fuck you, Julian.

GRAYLING: Hello!

SMITH: Welcome, all of you, to... the Brexit Club. Now I don't know why Theresa sent you to detention, and I don't care.

HAMMOND: This is *such* bullshit.

SMITH: Phil... Phil... Phil... Always playing the tough guy. Well, listen buddy, I'm the Chief Whip and you will respect me!

---

[*] Esther McVey would hold a number of ministerial positions throughout her career. She appears to have spent the early Brexit years bolstering her leadership credentials. She would be rewarded for this persistence by finishing last in the 2019 leadership election.

HAMMOND:	
SMITH:	
HAMMOND:	This is bullshit. Sir.
SMITH:	That's better. Now listen up, rejects. You are all mine for five hours. In that time, you will not talk to each other...
HAMMOND:	<Cough> *Fuckyou*. <Cough>
SMITH:	Got something to say to me, Hammond?
McVEY:	[Whispering] Phil! Stop provoking him!
WILLIAMSON:	[Whispering] For fuck's sake, Phil.
HAMMOND:	No.
SMITH:	
HAMMOND:	Sir.
SMITH:	Today, you will each write an essay. It will be called 'What Brexit means for the country'.
WILLIAMSON:	Mr Smith, sir, if I finish early, can I go?
RUDD:	Lol.
McVEY:	God, Gavin, you are such a nerd!
WILLIAMSON:	What?! It's a fair question.
SMITH:	No, Williamson. You cannot.
SMITH:	Now, I'll be in my office down the hall. But this door stays open! If I hear so much as a peep from this committee room, there'll be consequences. Clear?
WILLIAMSON/ RUDD/McVEY:	[Together] Yes, sir.
SMITH:	Hammond?
HAMMOND:	

SMITH:

HAMMOND: *Sir.*

[The committee room. Two minutes later]

HAMMOND: Okay, he's gone. I'm
                shutting the door.

WILLIAMSON: No! Mr Smith said not to!

HAMMOND: Gavin, two weeks ago you practically
                declared war on China. Are you really
                that scared of the Chief Whip?

McVEY: I don't like this either.

HAMMOND: Oh, for fuck's sake, I'll do
                it quietly.

<Click>

HAMMOND: There. So, come on, tell me. How did
                you lot offend the prime minister?

WILLIAMSON: We're meant to be writing
                our essays...

HAMMOND: Oh relax, Gavin. We're here for five
                hours. Let's chat.

McVEY: He's got a point.

HAMMOND: Bingo. See, Esther agrees and Chris
                does too, don't you?

GRAYLING: Sorry, what's happening?

HAMMOND: See?

HAMMOND: What about you Amber? Wanna chat?

RUDD: [Shrugging]

McVEY: You won't get anything out of her.

RUDD: [Sticking her tongue out]

133

McVEY:	See? She's been like this since last April.
WILLIAMSON:	Guys, someone's coming! Shush.

[Door opens]

MILIBAND:	Oh. Hello, everyone. Don't mind me.
EVERYONE:	<Giggles>
MILIBAND:	I'm just out for a stroll. You know, passing the time.
HAMMOND:	How *lovely* for you.
EVERYONE:	<Sniggers>
MILIBAND:	Ah... I see. It's like that, is it? Well, remember this: I used to be like you. I had dreams. I even had an 'Ed Stone'. But then, one day, I learned that I wasn't special. And neither are any of you.
EVERYONE:	
MILIBAND:	Remember this: however good things look to you now, however powerful you think you are, every MP is just one bad bacon butty away from the backbenches.
EVERYONE:	
MILIBAND:	Enjoy it while you can, kids.

[Two minutes later]

WILLIAMSON:	Okay, he's gone.
HAMMOND:	Well, that was sobering.
McVEY:	Is he right?
WILLIAMSON:	He can't be, right? We're different.
McVEY:	Yes!

HAMMOND: Yup. I'll never be like that.

RUDD: [Quietly] You're all wrong.

HAMMOND: She speaks!

RUDD: Only when I want to. And he's right.

HAMMOND: How can you know that?

RUDD: Two words: Windrush Scandal.

McVEY: Oh.

RUDD: Exactly.

———————————

[Two hours later]

WILLIAMSON: I'm hungry.

McVEY: Me too.

HAMMOND: Let's go to the Terrace Café.

WILLIAMSON: I don't know... Julian said to
              stay here.

HAMMOND: Stop worrying. It's the other way, so
              he won't see us. Trust me, I do it
              all the time.

McVEY: You're here a lot?

HAMMOND: Yup. So is Chris.

GRAYLING: Hello!

HAMMOND: That's the spirit, pal.

———————————

[The Terrace Café]

McVEY: This was a good call.

HAMMOND: Told you. So come on, spill. Why has
              Theresa given you detention?

McVEY:	You'll laugh...
HAMMOND:	We won't.
McVEY:	Promise?
WILLIAMSON:	Promise.
McVEY:	It was for founding Ladies For Leave.
RUDD:	Ha!
McVEY:	Hey! You promised!
HAMMOND:	[Pointing] He promised; she didn't.
WILLIAMSON:	Wait — Ladies For Leave is real?
McVEY:	Yes!
HAMMOND:	I'm with Gavin here. I assumed it was a massive troll.
McVEY:	Why does no one believe me?!
RUDD:	Lol.
HAMMOND:	Oh, come on. It *is* pretty funny.
McVEY:	It's real — why can no one accept this? I don't understand why everyone thinks that I was joking.
WILLIAMSON:	But Ladies For Leave, I mean...
McVEY:	Why is it so silly that I want a place where I can just chat to other ladies who like Brexit?
EVERYONE:	
McVEY:	Is that really so wrong?
HAMMOND:	I mean...
McVEY:	I just want a place to be me.
EVERYONE:	

McVEY: So come on then, Gavin, why are you here?

WILLIAMSON: I don't really...

McVEY: Come on. You laughed at me, but I told you.

HAMMOND: She's got a point.

McVEY: It's your turn. Why are you in detention?

WILLIAMSON: Okay! Fine! I... told the *Sun* I could send the army into London to stop knife crime.

McVEY: Wow.

WILLIAMSON: Look, it was stupid, I know, but I was angry! Flustered! I... wasn't thinking straight.

McVEY: Why?

WILLIAMSON: Because the other day, someone went into my office and broke all my Space Marines.

HAMMOND: Oh. *Oh*...

WILLIAMSON: Hmmm? What's that, Phil?

HAMMOND: Um... Nothing.

WILLIAMSON: You all think it's so easy to be Defence Secretary.

McVEY: Well it is, isn't it? Prance about in a flak jacket, don't lose the Falklands. It's not that hard.

WILLIAMSON: Look, the pressure is intense. I don't know anything about war. Not really. I wasn't a soldier! I sold fireplaces. Every night I have nightmares about looking shit in a tank.

WILLIAMSON: What about you then, Phil? Why are
                you in detention?

HAMMOND: Me? Oh, like I said, I'm here
                all the time.

McVEY: Don't dodge the question! Everyone
                else is 'fessing up. You have
                to as well.

HAMMOND: No, they aren't. Amber hasn't told us
                why she's—

RUDD: I'll tell you.

McVEY: What?

RUDD: I don't care. I'll tell you
                why I'm here.

WILLIAMSON: I think that's the most words you've
                said all day.

RUDD: Yeah, well, can you blame me? I see
                how you all look at me now.

WILLIAMSON: I don't—

RUDD: You look at me like I'm a basket
                case. None of you talk to me.

WILLIAMSON: I wasn't—

McVEY: I wouldn't—

RUDD: You don't. Don't lie about it. No one
                does. Not since Windrush. You all look
                at me like I'm damaged goods.

McVEY: Amber, I—

RUDD: You know what? I don't care what you
                think. That's the thing. I figured
                if everyone in the party thinks I'm
                damaged, then why hold back about how
                shit we are on unemployment benefits?
                I just say what I think now.

HAMMOND: [Muttering] Which has its problems...

RUDD: That was an accident!

138

HAMMOND: I'm just saying...

RUDD: Anyway, that's it. I say what I think,
              and the prime minister can't fire me
              for it. So she sends me here instead.

McVEY: Wait, what do you mean? *Of course* the
              prime minister could fire you!

RUDD: Nope. Think about it. Small majority,
              plus she needs MPs who'll respect the
              principle of collective ministerial
              responsibility. Do the maths. That
              leaves, like, twenty-seven people who
              can actually be ministers now.

WILLIAMSON: That can't be true...

RUDD: It is. Trust me. We're all safe, and
              your proof is sitting right there.

GRAYLING: Hello!

RUDD: Tell everyone why you're in
              detention, Chris.

GRAYLING: God, I don't know really. I mean,
              it's quite hard to narrow it down.

RUDD: Go on, have a go.

GRAYLING: Where to start, though?

HAMMOND: Maybe limit yourself to stuff from
              just this week?

GRAYLING: Okay, well this week it was revealed
              that I completely broke the probation
              system while at the Ministry of
              Justice. Then there's the whole ferries
              thing — that's kicked off again. Oh!
              And I accidentally went in the wrong
              voting lobby at one of the Brexit votes
              and voted against the prime minister.
              That was pretty bad. Then there's the
              EU shipping pallet shortage and...

McVEY:	Jesus Christ, Chris.
WILLIAMSON:	No wonder you're in detention.
GRAYLING:	Actually, I'm not finished yet! So... I also accidentally removed all the cheap rail fares in my own constituency. Then I tried to hide from the ferry debate in Parliament—
HAMMOND:	Is this going to take much longer? We've only got three hours left.
RUDD:	You see what I mean? If she can't fire Chris, then how can she fire any of us?
HAMMOND:	That is... a lot of fuck-ups, Chris.
GRAYLING:	Oh, I know.
McVEY:	You do?
GRAYLING:	Oh yes. I know you laugh at me, but it's not nice being bulletproof, you know.
WILLIAMSON:	Sorry, what?
GRAYLING:	I'd actually quite like to be fired.
McVEY:	You *want* to be fired?
GRAYLING:	Well, I *am* a bit rubbish, aren't I?
HAMMOND:	Well...
GRAYLING:	It just never seems to happen. Whenever I really muck something up, I get promoted. I just seem to fail upwards.
RUDD:	'The White Male's Burden.' Oh, you *poor* thing...
GRAYLING:	Of course, what I'd really like to do is drive lorries.
WILLIAMSON:	You want to be a lorry driver?

GRAYLING: Oh yes. I'm actually quite good at it, you know.

HAMMOND: To be fair, he is.

GRAYLING: Thank you.

HAMMOND: Ten four, good buddy.

GRAYLING: Actually, that doesn't mean...

HAMMOND: Just take the fucking compliment, Chris.

RUDD: Well, I'm terribly sorry that you're suffering due to society's addiction to promoting crap white men, Chris.

GRAYLING: Thank you, Amber, that does help.

RUDD: I didn't mean that as a...

GRAYLING: Hmm?

RUDD: ... Never mind.

WILLIAMSON: Go on then, Phil. Your turn. Why are you in detention?

HAMMOND: You don't want to know.

WILLIAMSON: Yes I do.

HAMMOND: Nope.

McVEY: We've all 'fessed up!

RUDD: Don't be a coward. You have to spill too.

HAMMOND: Well, okay. Now remember, Gavin, you asked for this... I'm here because Theresa found out I broke your Space Marines.

WILLIAMSON: That was you?! *You utter shit!*

HAMMOND: Hey!

WILLIAMSON: *You broke my Space Marines!!*

McVEY:	Gavin! Keep your voice down!
HAMMOND:	You deserved it. After that crap you caused with China...
WILLIAMSON:	The Ultragavines were a custom Space Marine chapter! I'd written extensive lore! I spent *months* coming up with a backstory for Primarch Gavinus!
HAMMOND:	Gavin, this conversation isn't making me regret my decision.
WILLIAMSON:	*They had custom rank insignia, Phil!*
RUDD:	Gavin! Stop shouting!
SMITH:	[From nearby] Hey! What's going on over there?!
McVEY:	Shit! Smith heard us!
HAMMOND:	
WILLIAMSON:	The Chief Whip's coming! We're so fucked...
HAMMOND:	
RUDD:	What are we going to do?!
HAMMOND:	Ah, fuck it. Stay here and stay quiet. I'll distract him and lead him in the other direction.
RUDD:	What?!
HAMMOND:	Look, he hates me anyway. Just wait here.
McVEY:	Phil!
HAMMOND:	Run back to the committee room when he's gone. Don't leave Chris behind.
GRAYLING:	Hello!

[A Parliamentary corridor]

SMITH: Damn ministers... What's going on
                out here...

HAMMOND: [Runs past singing] I don't know but
                I've been told/Julian Smith broke the
                pairing code!/In Commons votes it's
                plain to see!/Julian Smith couldn't
                even whip cream!

SMITH: [Chasing] *Hammond, you little shit,
                come here!!*

                              ————————

[Back in the committee room. Five minutes later]

SMITH: [Slamming door] Now get back in there
                and finish that goddamn essay!

RUDD: He caught you?

HAMMOND: [Sitting down] Yeah, he's
                surprisingly fast.

McVEY: Why did you do that? Why did you
                cover for us? You didn't have to.

HAMMOND:

GRAYLING: Oh, Phil's really quite a nice man.
                He just won't admit it.

HAMMOND: Shut up, Chris.

                              ————————

RUDD: So what do we do about this essay?

HAMMOND: I say we let Gavin write it. For
                all of us.

McVEY: Agreed.

WILLIAMSON: Really? You're all fine with that?
                Are you sure?

143

HAMMOND:	And... Look, I'm sorry about your Space Marines.
WILLIAMSON:	Thanks, Phil. I know that you wouldn't do it again.
HAMMOND:	Oh Gavin, we both know that's not true.

[Committee room. Later. Smith enters. There is a single essay on the table]

Dear Mr Smith.

We accept that we had to sacrifice a Saturday in detention for whatever it was we did wrong. But we think you're crazy to make us write an essay telling you what we think Brexit means.

Because we found out today that we're all just ministers in Theresa May's Government of Dunning-Krugerland. We're all a geek...

McVEY:	A princess...
RUDD:	A basket case...
HAMMOND:	A rebel...
GRAYLING:	... and a Grayling.

And what we learned today was that there's one thing we all believe:

Brexit means Brexit.[*]

[*] It seems a successful film was later made about the events that Saturday, recounted here. Although names and other elements appear to have been changed for dramatic purposes.

CHAPTER SEVENTEEN

DOWNINGFALL

By spring 2019 the prime minister had become increasingly frustrated at her own party's lack of cooperation. This led to a number of odd speeches and outbursts to the press. After multiple failures to get her deal past the House of Commons, in the depths of Parliament, the prime minister lashed out at those around her...

[In the Cabinet]

HAMMOND: Those opposed to your deal have
             broken our unity in the House. On
             our own benches, our opponents have
             taken Grieve and are pushing Letwin.*
             There's resistance on the opposition
             benches between SNP and Labour, and
             elsewhere Remainism is entrenched in
             the Independent Group too.

MAY: Everything will be fine after
             Meaningful Vote Three.

HAMMOND: *Mein* Prime Minister... John Bercow...

LIDINGTON: Bercow has blocked another vote.
             Without significant changes, it will
             not occur.

---

* Late in her premiership, resistance to Theresa May's Brexit deal within her own party coalesced around MPs such as Dominic Grieve and Oliver Letwin, who believed it would lead to a hard Brexit. Lord Johnson would withdraw the whip from these MPs, amidst claims of fearmongering, before proceeding to deliver a hard Brexit.

MAY: These people will stay: Gove, Hammond,
                Lidington and Rudd.

                _____

MAY: [Shouting] That was an order!
                Meaningful Vote Three was an order!
                Who the *hell* do you all think
                you are, that you dare to resist
                my orders?

<Fist slams on desk>

MAY: Is this what it has come to?!
                Parliament has lied to me! Everyone
                has lied to me, even my own MPs!
                All of you, including my Cabinet
                ministers, are nothing but a bunch of
                wicked, faithless cowards!

LIDINGTON: *Mein* Prime Minister! I cannot allow
                you to insult your ministers and the
                MPs who have voted for you...

MAY: You are *cowards, traitors*
                and failures!

LIDINGTON: *Mein* Prime Minister, what you're
                saying is monstrous!

MAY: MPs are the *scum* of the British people
                right now! You have no honour! You
                call yourselves 'Cabinet ministers',
                but that's only because you have spent
                years in Parliament learning how to
                hold pointless debates.

MAY: I never studied PPE[*] and yet, alone,
                all by myself, I have negotiated a deal
                with Europe. All of you are traitors.
                For *too many years* now Parliament has
                prevented my actions. It has put every
                conceivable *obstacle* in my way!

[*]   Studying Philosphy, Politics and Economics at Oxbridge appears to have been a popular
      choice for the Brexit generation of MPs. Historians have long debated whether the purpose
      of this degree was to teach them these things, or rob them of any understanding of them.
      Based on their behaviour in government, modern thinking leans towards the latter.

MAY: I would have done well to have fired
                all my ministers years ago. You think
                Putin puts up with this?!

MAY: [Shouting] *From the very beginning I
                have been betrayed and deceived by
                Parliament!*

MAY: What a monstrous betrayal of the
                British people! But all of you — the
                traitors, the MPs — will pay. *You
                shall pay yourselves and be voted out!*

[Outside the room. Stephen is crying]

FOX: It's okay, Stephen. Calm down!

[Inside]

MAY: My orders are lost to the wind.
                It is impossible to lead in these
                circumstances. It is over. This
                war is lost. But if you think I'll
                vacate this office, you are very
                much mistaken!

EVERYONE:

MAY: I would rather put a bullet through
                the economy. Do what you want now. Go.

[Outside Downing Street. Shortly afterwards]

HAMMOND: What the *fuck* was that all about?

LIDINGTON: I don't... she can't...

RUDD: Michael, how are you so calm?

GOVE: hMM? oH. I wAS JuST reMEMbeRING THaT
               I wAs iN thE RooM wHEn sOmEONe gAvE
               thAT spEEch befORE.

HAMMOND: You were?

GOVE: oH yES. anD iT sOUNdeD muCH beTTer iN
               tHE OrIGINal GerMAN.

CHAPTER EIGHTEEN

MAULED BY EWOKS

In March 2019, after a second failure to force a vote on her Withdrawal Agreement in Parliament, the prime minister renewed her efforts to get it through one more time. A serious barrier remained. This was the enforcement, by the Speaker, of the rule that no bill can be debated multiple times without significant changes...

_____

[A Cabinet meeting]

MAY: So how do I get Meaningful Vote Three past Bercow?

LIDINGTON: We're trying again?

MAY: Yes. Think of this as my *Return of the Jedi* moment.

HAMMOND: It does feel like we're being repeatedly mauled by Ewoks.[*]

LEADSOM: Why are you here, Phil? Don't you hate this plan?

HAMMOND: Fuck knows. I've no idea any more.

_____

_____

[*] One of the interesting things the tapes often do is remind us of how different things were in the past. It's worth remembering that to our ancestors Disney was still just a media company, not a country.

LIDINGTON: What if we change the font size?
              Would that count as a significant
              difference?

LEADSOM: We already used that for
              Meaningful Vote Two.

LIDINGTON: Ah.

MAY: We could attach it to a
              regret motion?[*]

HAMMOND: Well, we've certainly got plenty
              of those...

MAY: Can you at least *pretend* to be helpful?

MAY: Okay, what about separating the deal
              from the political declaration on the
              Irish border?

LIDINGTON: Can we do that?

LEADSOM: I don't know.

HAMMOND: Are you mad? The DUP will roast you.

MAY: But will it work? Where's Michael?
              Devious plans are his *modus operandi*.

HAMMOND: At the ERG. It's Thatcher
              Fanfic Friday.

[At the ERG. The same time]

BAKER: Thatcher locked eyes with him across
              the table. 'Oh, so that's how you like
              it?' she said, towering over him. 'Well,
              maybe I should be Maa*strict* with you.'

HAMMOND: [On the phone] Michael, you there?

---

[*] A motion to regret was a mechanism that allowed MPs to attach a new motion to an existing bill. As with everything from this period, it seemed to involve no requirement to express or feel genuine regret.

GOVE:	bE quiCk. ThIS iS geTTInG gOOd.
HAMMOND:	The PM needs you here.
GOVE:	Is GrAYLinG thERe wITh yOU?
HAMMOND:	Yes.
GOVE:	tHeN... nO. I WIll nOt cOMe.

HAMMOND:	Gove won't come while Chris is here.
GRAYLING:	Hello!
MAY:	Why?
HAMMOND:	Honestly? I'm not sure. But he's been weird ever since Chris got that comfort duck.
M'GREH:	quACk
LEADSOM:	Why *is* Chris here?
MAY:	It's a secret.
GRAYLING:	Theresa is grooming me to be the next prime minister!
HAMMOND:	*Fucking what?!*
MAY:	Damn it, Chris.
LEADSOM:	*Chris* is your planned successor?!
MAY:	Yes.
LIDINGTON:	That's *crazy*! No offence.
GRAYLING:	None taken.
LEADSOM:	The duck would be better. No offence.
GRAYLING:	None taken.
HAMMOND:	It's like putting Pooh Bear in charge of a honey factory! No offence.
GRAYLING:	Okay, I *am* getting a little offended now.

LIDINGTON:	Chris *cannot* succeed you.
MAY:	He will continue my legacy.
HAMMOND:	Well, he *is* good at fucking things up...
GRAYLING:	Definitely offended now.
LIDINGTON:	Theresa! No!
MAY:	Well, would *you* take the job?
LIDINGTON:	Prime Minister! I... no.
MAY:	Exactly. Then it's Chris.
HAMMOND:	I suddenly understand how Albert Speer must have felt.

MAY:	Look. We separate the Northern Ireland border arrangement from the main deal and I quit. Boris and Jacob have agreed they'll back it.
HAMMOND:	Boris told you that, did he?
MAY:	Yes. Last night.
HAMMOND:	Might want to check today's paper. He's already briefing against you.
MAY:	That slippery *fuck*.
LEADSOM:	To be fair, seven hours of loyalty is a new personal best for him.
MAY:	Okay, fine. Well, we've still got Jacob. He'll—
HAMMOND:	Hang on, Gove is calling... Hello?
GOVE:	[On the phone, whispering] sTiLL wiTH thE PM?
HAMMOND:	Yup.
GOVE:	KeEP qUIeT. I'm PuTTIng yOU oN sPeaKER.

[The ERG meeting]

BAKER: ... and we will NOT be cowed!
                  Liberty! Egality! Grand wizardry!

ERG: *Huzzah!*

BAKER: Were the British cowed by the Normans?

GOVE: eRM...

ERG: *No!*

BAKER: Did the British not stand *alone*
                  against the French at Waterloo?!

GOVE: nOt rEAlly. The gERMaNs, dUTch and
                  BeLGIAns...

ERG: *Yes!*

BAKER: Did the British not win a glorious
                  victory at Dunkirk?!

GOVE: Oh, CoME oN...

ERG: *Yes!*

BAKER: *We will fight to the end on the*
                  Beaches of Brexit!

ERG: *HUZZAH!*

HAMMOND: Sounds like that's the ERG out.

MAY: Shit.

LEADSOM: Pull the vote?

MAY: No. It can still get through.

LIDINGTON: How?

MAY: We just need enough Labour rebels.

HAMMOND: You're relying on Corbyn being shit
                  at whipping?

MAY: Yup.

HAMMOND: That's... actually not the worst plan.

MAY: Indeed.

CHAPTER NINETEEN

MY WAY OR THE HUAWEI

As things began to fall apart for the prime minister, some of her Cabinet sensed weakness and started to brief against her. One of those was Gavin Williamson, who wasn't quite as careful as he should have been in conversations with journalists. Allegedly.

[Downing Street]

WILLIAMSON: You wanted to see me?

MAY: Yes, Gavin, I did. Come in.

WILLIAMSON:

MAY:

WILLIAMSON: Is... this... about me trying to name a submarine HMS *Rogal Dorn*?

MAY: No, Gavin. Somewhat incredibly, it is not. Anything else spring to mind?

WILLIAMSON:

MAY:

WILLIAMSON: Is it about that time a month ago when I threatened to go to war with China, and they banned Phil Hammond from entering the country in revenge?

MAY: Nope.

WILLIAMSON: Oh.

MAY:	I'll be honest, that was actually pretty funny. Keep thinking, Gavin.
WILLIAMSON:	Hmmm... Is it... about the time I claimed I could send the army into London to stop knife crime?
MAY:	No. Again, bizarrely, it is not. You already did detention for that one.
WILLIAMSON:	Or... when I told everyone I was going to create a Royal Drone Force?[*]
MAY:	Still no.
WILLIAMSON:	Is this about bringing an air rifle to Chequers?
MAY:	God. I'd forgotten that one.
WILLIAMSON:	Or...
MAY:	Huawei, Gavin.
WILLIAMSON:	What?
MAY:	I know about Huawei.[†]
WILLIAMSON:	I don't know what you're talking abo—
MORDAUNT:	[Entering] Hello, Gavin.
WILLIAMSON:	What's Penny doing here?
MAY:	You leaked, Gavin. Leaky McLeaked.
WILLIAMSON:	I didn't! I didn't!
MAY:	It's time to go, Gavin.
WILLIAMSON:	But you can't! Who could replace..? Oh no, not Penny. You can't! She's... I mean, you can see that... She's a... a...
MORDAUNT:	... Serving naval reservist?
MAY:	Take him away, Penny.

[*] One of the questions the tapes finally, definitively answered was who first had the idea for the Royal Drone Force. This is why a bronze statue of Williamson was recently unveiled in front of their headquarters in Oxford.

[†] IT self-service seems to have been a major obsession for our ancestors. Bizarrely, this seems to have regularly extended to offering to install their own spyware.

WILLIAMSON: I'm innocent! You can't do this!

HAMMOND: <Whistles jauntily>

STEPHEN: Why are you so happy?

HAMMOND: Who? Me? No reason.

STEPHEN: It's very suspicious.

HAMMOND: What?! I can't just be happy
                sometimes?

STEPHEN: Phil, the only other times I've seen
                you this happy are when you're drunk,
                or when Microsoft add new formula
                features to Excel.

HAMMOND: Can't a man just be happy?

STEPHEN: In *this* government? No.

HAMMOND: Maybe I'm just having a happy day.

STEPHEN: That sounds staggeringly unlikely.

[Outside the office]

WILLIAMSON: [Screaming] *I'm innocent!*
                I'm innocent!

MORDAUNT: Come on now, Gavin. Don't make
                a fuss. You're only embarrassing
                yourself here.

STEPHEN: Is that Gavin being dragged away?

HAMMOND: [Chuckling] Yup!

STEPHEN: Phil... what did you do?!

HAMMOND: Me?! Nothing, honest. Hmmm... Wonder
                how much plane tickets to China are
                right now...

STEPHEN: [Suspicious] Phil—

WILLIAMSON:	Oh, thank God. Guys, you *have* to hide me! I managed to escape, but Penny's right behind me!
STEPHEN:	What did you do?!
WILLIAMSON:	Nothing! I'm innocent!
HAMMOND:	I find that very hard to believe.
WILLIAMSON:	You *have* to believe me. *Please.* Hide me!
STEPHEN:	*Gah.* Fine. Quick, get under the desk.

[Two minutes later]

MORDAUNT:	You two seen Gavin anywhere?
STEPHEN:	Not recently.
HAMMOND:	He's under the desk.
MORDAUNT:	Cheers.
STEPHEN:	Phil!
HAMMOND:	What?

WILLIAMSON:	[Crying] *I'm innocent!*
MORDAUNT:	Stop struggling.
WILLIAMSON:	[Shouting] Stephen! Phil! Save my Ultragavines! They're in my office! Don't let Penny touch them! She won't play them properly! *She hasn't read my lore guide! She won't..!*

[Door slams]

STEPHEN:	What's an Ultragavine?!
HAMMOND:	His custom *Warhammer* army.
STEPHEN:	Christ.

CHAPTER TWENTY

TO THE FUBARBUNKER!

As the prime minister attempted to negotiate a deal with Labour to get her Brexit agreement through Parliament, resignations and sackings from her government became a daily activity. Despite her determination to hold on, the ministerial shelves were getting bare...

[Parliament. Lidington's office]

LIDINGTON: Right. The PM says we need to find some new ministers.

HAMMOND: Is there anyone left?

LIDINGTON: It's fine. Gove gave me a list of possible candid— Hey! Give that back! What are you...?

HAMMOND: [Flicking his lighter] I'm burning it.

LIDINGTON: Why?!

HAMMOND: Because *Michael Gove wrote it.*

LIDINGTON: Oh. Right. Good point.

HAMMOND: How come we got hunt-the-minister duty anyway?

LIDINGTON: It was this or help at that summit meeting she's holding with the Labour leadership to try and get their votes.

HAMMOND: Jesus.

LIDINGTON: Exactly. You can thank me later.

HAMMOND: Who drew that straw?

————————————————

[Downing Street. The same time]

MAY:

CORBYN:

MAY:

STEPHEN: Um. So... Did anyone see *Fleabag*
                last night?

MAY:

CORBYN:

MAY:

STEPHEN: That's a 'no', then?

MAY:

CORBYN:

MAY:

STEPHEN: So...

CORBYN:

MAY:

STEPHEN: Um.

CORBYN:

MAY:

STEPHEN: Tea, anyone?

CORBYN:

MAY:

STEPHEN: Or coffee?

MAY:

CORBYN:

STEPHEN: We have the cool coffee. The kind
                that comes in those little pots you
                put in a machine. Anyone?[*]

MAY:

CORBYN:

[Door opens]

STARMER: Sorry I'm late! Did I miss anything?!

STEPHEN: Oh, thank *God*.

MAY:

CORBYN:

STEPHEN: [Aside] Is yours normally like this?

STARMER: [Aside] Oh yes.

CORBYN:

MAY:

STARMER: He's... enigmatic. Yours?

MAY:

CORBYN:

STEPHEN: Well, she's been under a lot
                of pressure.

MAY:

CORBYN:

STEPHEN: How have you been, anyway?

STARMER: Hmm? Oh me? Not bad. Not bad.

STEPHEN: Cool.

---

[*] Stratified layers of tiny coffee pots have become one of the most useful tools for archaeologists in dating ancient burials and buildings from the twenty-first century.

162

[In Whitehall. The same time]

HAMMOND: So how many new ministers do we need?

LIDINGTON: Four.

HAMMOND: No ERG. No Remainers. No leadership
                candidates... fucking hell.

LIDINGTON: It can't be that hard.

HAMMOND: We're playing Shit MP Guess Who here,
                David. And we've already flipped
                down Gavin Williamson, Liz Truss and
                Chris Grayling.

HAMMOND: Robin Walker?

LIDINGTON: Got.

HAMMOND: Nusrat Ghani?

LIDINGTON: Got.

HAMMOND: Will Quince?

LIDINGTON: Don't got.

HAMMOND: Thank fu—

LIDINGTON: No, wait. My bad. He's at Work
                and Pensions.

HAMMOND: Shit. John Glen? Isn't that a dead
                astronaut? Is Grant Shapps up to his
                old tricks again?

LIDINGTON: Nope, he's real. MP for Salisbury.
                Got, though. He's one of yours,
                apparently. Treasury.

HAMMOND: Really? Huh.

HAMMOND: Chloe Smith?

LIDINGTON: Got.

HAMMOND: Shailesh Vara?

LIDINGTON: Don't got. Sounds familiar, though.

HAMMOND: Not to me.

LIDINGTON: Yeah... wait. I'm going to look
him up. Hah!

HAMMOND: What?

LIDINGTON: Hmm? Oh, ignore me. Just memories.

HAMMOND: Got or not got?

LIDINGTON: Probably best to scratch him
off the list.

[Downing Street. The same time]

STARMER: B7.

MAY:

CORBYN:

STEPHEN: Hit.

MAY:

CORBYN:

STARMER: Lovely stuff! B8.

MAY:

CORBYN:

STEPHEN: Ha! Miss. D4.

MAY:

CORBYN:

STARMER: Miss. C7.

MAY:

CORBYN:

STEPHEN: Hit! Bugger. You sunk my
battleship. A2.

MAY:

CORBYN:

STARMER: Miss. F2.

MAY:

CORBYN:

STEPHEN: Miss. E6.

MAY:

CORBYN:

[In Whitehall]

HAMMOND: Kelly Tolhurst?

LIDINGTON: Got.

HAMMOND: Jesse Norman?

LIDINGTON: Got. Why is finding new
              ministers so hard?

HAMMOND: The PM keeps being outwitted by Magic
              Granddad, an MP who looks like he
              should be teaching Japanese kids maths
              on a Nintendo DS. It's hardly an
              incentive to serve, is it?

HAMMOND: Mims Davies?

LIDINGTON: Got.

HAMMOND: James Cleverly?

LIDINGTON:

HAMMOND: I said: 'James Cleverly'.

LIDINGTON: I know... I'm just looking... I can't
              see him... yes! Don't got! Don't
              got, Phil!

HAMMOND: Thank *fuck*. Finally.

LIDINGTON: So, what do we know about
              James Cleverly?

HAMMOND:	Looking now... Not much. Ex-London Assembly. Hmmm, he does have a controversy section on Wikipedia...
LIDINGTON:	Oh?
HAMMOND:	Looks like he called Simon Hughes a dick, once.
LIDINGTON:	That's controversial?
HAMMOND:	Apparently.
LIDINGTON:	Wow.
HAMMOND:	I know. It's not like it would be hard to find a cite.

[Downing Street]

MAY:	
CORBYN:	
STEPHEN:	Sorry, but Pacey and Joey was just wrong.
MAY:	
CORBYN:	
STARMER:	What?! How can you *possibly* have shipped Doey?!
MAY:	
CORBYN:	
STEPHEN:	Because Dawson's name was in the title. It was *Dawson*'s Creek.
MAY:	
CORBYN:	
STARMER:	Why does that matter?
MAY:	
CORBYN:	

STEPHEN: The show was about *Dawson*.

MAY:

CORBYN:

STARMER: Sure, that may have been the
             intention. But it quickly grew beyond
             that and became an ensemble piece.
             Plus, PJ just worked better. The
             chemistry was obvious.[*]

MAY:

CORBYN:

STEPHEN: I won't deny they had chemistry.
             I'm just...

CORBYN:

MAY:

STEPHEN: These talks aren't going
             anywhere, are they?

STARMER: Not really, no.

HAMMOND: That's it. We've run out of MPs.

LIDINGTON: But we still need more ministers...

HAMMOND: We have scraped the bottom of
             the barrel! The young and the
             old have been conscripted!
             Götterdowningrung is now!

LIDINGTON: You're being a tad dramatic, Phil.

HAMMOND: Come, David! To the FUBARbunker! Let
             us go parade our final cohort in
             front of the prime minister before
             the Russians arrive...

---

[*] It was only in the late twenty-fifth century that historians finally concluded that Doey was,
in fact, the definitive *Dawson's Creek* 'ship.

CHAPTER TWENTY-ONE

HMS *KING GEORGE VI*

Defence Secretary Penny Mordaunt was a naval reservist and long-time supporter of the military. With the prime minister and Treasury focused on economic impact forecasts for Brexit, she was given the freedom to take a more hands-on approach to the department's operational management than previous office holders.

MORDAUNT:[*]   Okay. I've looked at the list of names you've suggested for our newest submarine, and I have question.

FIRST LORD: Oh no...

MORDAUNT: Why is there an appendix on naming submarines after... what does it say here... 'Space Marines'?

FIRST LORD: Ah. Right. So, Minister, have you heard of Rogal Dorn?

MORDAUNT: Royal Dawn?

FIRST LORD: No, Rogal Dorn.

MORDAUNT: What's a Rogal Dorn?

FIRST LORD: Apparently, he's a hero of the Imperium.

MORDAUNT: The British Empire?

FIRST LORD: No, the Imperium of Man.

[*] 'Due to her service and experience, Mordaunt proved to be a particularly effective Secretary of Defence and Cabinet minister. This is probably why Lord Johnson almost immediately fired her.' Kelly Welles, *Fear and Loathing in the Palace of Westminster*

MORDAUNT: I am *beyond* lost here.

FIRST LORD: Okay, let me explain.

MORDAUNT: Do you have to?

FIRST LORD: Right. In *Warhammer 40K*, which is set
               in space and in the future—

MORDAUNT: So... science fiction?

FIRST LORD: No, apparently not. Your predecessor
               was very insistent on this.

MORDAUNT: Oh God, *of course*, this is a
               Gavin thing.

FIRST LORD: Anyway, Rogal Dorn was Primarch of
               the Imperial Fists.

MORDAUNT: Prime of the what now?

FIRST LORD: Primarch of the Imperial Fists. A sort
               of founder of a future military order.
               Gavin insisted he was the best, which
               is why the Ultragavines chapter are...

MORDAUNT: The what? Chapter what?

FIRST LORD: Okay let me explain chapters.

MORDAUNT: Chapters?

FIRST LORD: So, Space Marines are divided into
               chapters these—

MORDAUNT: First Lord, is there any way, I
               stress *any* way, we can skip to the
               end of this conversation?

FIRST LORD: Oh. Right. Short version is that
               Gavin tried to name a submarine HMS
               Rogal Dorn.

MORDAUNT: Right. Of course he fucking did.

———————————

MORDAUNT: So this is why the Royal Navy intranet now has an entire subsection dedicated to the *Warhammer* universe?

FIRST LORD: Yes, Minister. Now, as you'll see here from my list, a number of non-Primarchs *would* match our naming criteria and—

MORDAUNT: First Lord?

FIRST LORD: Minister?

MORDAUNT: How about we *don't* name submarines after Space Marines?

FIRST LORD: Oh, thank God. Thank you, Minister.

MORDAUNT: Are you... crying, First Lord?

FIRST LORD: No, Minister. It's just... dusty in here. How would you feel about HMS *King George VI*?

MORDAUNT: Perfect. Let's keep the science-fiction and computer games out of the navy, shall we?

FIRST LORD: Thank you. Goodbye, Minister.

[Door closes]

MORDAUNT: Have you played the new *World of Warships* update yet?!

GOVE: [On Discord] nO.

MORDAUNT: It's sooo good!

CHAPTER TWENTY-TWO

THE FALL

On 23 May 2019, after a catastrophic set of results in the European elections, Theresa May stood at the podium outside Number 10 and resigned as prime minister.

[Entering Downing Street]

MAY: Well, that's it. It's done.

LIDINGTON:

MAY:

LIDINGTON: Fucking hell.

MAY: Don't swear, David.

LIDINGTON: Sorry.

CHAPTER TWENTY-THREE

CLEARING OUT THE OFFICE

After Theresa May's resignation, a short period of peace reigned in Whitehall as those loyal to her began to face the future, and those disloyal began to openly jockey for power.

————————

[Downing Street]

HAMMOND: Clearing out the office?

MAY: Phil! Yes.

HAMMOND: Hard, isn't it? I've been doing the same. Thought I'd stop by and see if you needed a hand.

MAY: You don't think you'll be staying on?

HAMMOND: Have you seen who's running for Tory leader? No fucking chance.

MAY: You're not running yourself?

HAMMOND: God, no.

MAY: I assume Michael is?

HAMMOND: So he says, but...

MAY: But what?

HAMMOND: I don't know. It's odd. He just didn't seem his usual self when we spoke about it.

————————

[Deep under the ocean. The same time]

THE OLD ONES: <Unnatural screams>

GOVE: I jUSt... I WOndEReD iF I cOUld sIT
            tHIs oNE oUT.

THE OLD ONES: <Vast clicking>

GOVE: yES, I kNOw. BuT I'd jUSt beEN
            nOMiNAteD to CHaIR tHe viLLaGE
            RaMBLiNG clUB tHIs yEaR.

THE OLD ONES: <Death rattle>

GOVE: It'S a HuGE hONouR.

THE OLD ONES: <Silent screams>

GOVE: aND iT'S nOt LiKe tHEY aREn'T SoWInG
            eNOUgh ChAOs thEMselVEs Up THeRE
            rIGht nOw...

[Downing Street]

MAY: You're not the only one to say that.
            David was here earlier and said the
            same thing.

HAMMOND: I assume he's quitting too?

MAY: Yes. A lot of the old guard are. This
            is potentially a turning point in the
            Tory party, I think. And it's been
            coming for a long time. David Gauke[*]
            is already booking committee rooms for
            'resistance meetings'.

HAMMOND: Do resistance groups normally have
            official, minuted meetings?

MAY: I think he's quite new to this. But
            it's sweet that he's trying.

[*] The MP for Hertfordshire South West emerged as an unlikely leader of the Conservative opposition to hard Brexit. His leadership of the 'Gaukeward Squad' would prove to be more enthusiastic than successful.

HAMMOND: Still, part of me is very much
              looking forward to returning to the
              back benches.

MAY: Why?

HAMMOND: There's a sense of freedom there. You
              get to say what you think without the
              worry of being fired.

MAY: And that's different from how you were
              with me *how?*

HAMMOND:

MAY:

HAMMOND: Okay, fair point.

MAY: It is going to be very different
              though, isn't it?

HAMMOND: I suspect so. For a start—

WILLIAMSON: Theresa! I just heard! I just
              wanted to pop by and say how *sorry*
              I am that—

MAY: Gavin, if you do not leave this
              office immediately, I'm going to shove
              a pen right up your arse.

WILLIAMSON: Righto!

[Door slams]

MAY: Ghastly little weasel.

HAMMOND: One who is destined for great things,
              I suspect. And he won't be the only
              one. The future is not looking bright.

MAY: Is he running?

HAMMOND: I don't think so — Gavin is one of
              life's henchmen. Neither is Priti Patel.

MAY: Priti's not running?

HAMMOND: I doubt it. It's too early for her.
She needs to find some more immigrants
to shout at first. Maybe make a few
speeches where she suggests bringing
back hanging.

MAY: Ah. The classics.

HAMMOND: Like Gavin, she'll focus on buttering
up the winner this time around.
Get some more *Daily Mail*[*] time
under her belt.

MAY: Do you know what, Phil, I think
this might be the only sinking ship
where the rats aren't fleeing —
they're boarding.

MAY: Do you ever wonder how it all
went wrong?

HAMMOND: Not really. That's obvious. I
hope David Cameron's posh shed
collapses on him.

MAY: No, I mean after that. For
me. For us.

HAMMOND: Well, declaring forty-eight per
cent of the people in this country
'citizens of nowhere' probably wasn't
the greatest start.

MAY: Oh, very funny. I do wonder though
whether we ever had a chance to
pull this off.

HAMMOND: Does it matter? It's all immaterial now.

MAY: I just keep thinking about something
you said to me a long time ago.

HAMMOND: That we're fucked? I believe I even
underlined it.

---

[*] The *Daily Mail* was a curious publication. Those copies that have been found seem to primarily focus on what our ancestors thought would, or would not, give them cancer. Sometimes things that apparently did both at the same time.

175

MAY: No, that sometimes leadership means
              admitting there *isn't* a third way.

HAMMOND: Oh. That.

MAY: Turns out you were right.
              There wasn't.

MAY: So what happens next? Who do you
              think will win?

HAMMOND: It'll be Boris.

MAY: God, I hope not. I hope it's
              someone sensible.

HAMMOND: [Sighing] Theresa, is there *anything*
              that's happened in the last three
              years which suggests that this
              party... that this *country* is capable
              of being sensible? Boris will lie,
              he will cheat and he will play to
              the devils of our worst nature. And
              they'll all cheer him for it, you
              know. Public and party. *You* were the
              sensible one. And you fucked it up.
              You *fucked it*, Theresa.

MAY:

HAMMOND:

MAY: Phil, I'm going to miss our
              conversations.

HAMMOND: Yeah. Me too.

CHAPTER TWENTY-FOUR

THE HUSTINGS

In the wake of the prime minister's resignation, the jockeying began in earnest for the leadership of the Conservative Party. The country watched to see who would manoeuvre themselves into office as the new prime minister.

[A committee room in Westminster]

JAVID: Gentlemen, the Saj suggests that we jointly announce that we will be fighting a clean leadership campaign.

RAAB: I'm confused. Why?

JAVID: To make all the other fuckers look dirty.

HANCOCK: Nice. I like it.

RAAB: I'm just not sure we should we be working together.

JAVID: It's in all our interests. We're not the leading pack, are we?

HANCOCK: He's right, Dom. Gove? Johnson? They're Champions League. We're barely pushing for Europe.

RAAB: I don't want Europe! No deal!

JAVID: Matt, don't confuse him.

RAAB: Why should I cooperate with you? I'm out near the front!

HANCOCK: Oh, Dom. You've never done a Tory
              leadership race, have you?[*]

JAVID: It's like the Grand National, Dom,
              but with even more runners.

HANCOCK: And deaths.

JAVID: And, most importantly, the front
              runners rarely win. Case in point: do
              you know how Thatcher became party
              leader, Dom?

RAAB: [Wistfully] There was a prophecy, long
              told in Conservative clubs, that one
              day a wise leader would—

HANCOCK: It was because Airey Neave was a
              devious shit.

JAVID: Bingo!

RAAB: What?

HANCOCK: Airey Neave knew Edward Heath would
              likely win the challenge to his
              leadership. Thatcher was seen as
              having no path to victory.

JAVID: So, Neave started telling Tory MPs
              individually to secretly vote for
              Thatcher 'as a protest vote'.[†]

HANCOCK: And enough did so that she actually
              won the first ballot.

RAAB: I don't get it. How did no one
              realise what was happening, that *loads*
              of MPs were now going to protest-vote
              for Thatcher at the same time?

HANCOCK: Because we're the *Tories*, Dom.

JAVID: Airey Neave knew that the only time
              we ever chat to each other is if
              we're shagging or stabbing.

---

[*] 'After the ban on fox hunting, Tory leadership contests became the blood sport of choice for
     most of the British aristocracy.' Teresa Edwards, *Pride and Peerages*
[†] Protest voting seems to have been a way our ancestors justified voting for things they
     wanted, but didn't want people to *know* that they wanted.

179

RAAB: Oh.

RAAB: But Thatcher was the Messiah! They
               taught us that in Young Conservatives!

JAVID: Well, that was true from a certain
               point of view.

RAAB: Certain point of view?

JAVID: Dom, you will find many of the truths
               Tories hold dear depend on a certain
               point of view.

HANCOCK: 'Brexit means Brexit.'

JAVID: Exactly. All we're saying, Dom, is
               you need allies.

RAAB:

HANCOCK: And well, it's us or...

—————————

[A car park beneath the Commons. The same time]

RORY STEWART:*You want some of these?

JAMES   Sure. Hey, these are pretty tasty.
CLEVERLY:

KIT   Gentlemen, the crumbs are damaging my
MALTHOUSE: interior.†

STEWART: Blimey, this car can talk.

KIT: Yes. And compromise.

CLEVERLY: Woah.

STEWART: So wait, you're running for Tory
               leader too?

KIT: Yes.

---

*   An experienced former soldier, diplomat and administrator in Iraq, Rory Stewart had
    considerable experience finding pragmatic solutions to complex problems. He was swiftly
    rejected as a suitable party leader by the Conservative Party base.
†   There is some confusion in the sources as to whether Kit Malthouse was the same sentient
    car that TV evidence suggests wandered the US, fighting crime, in the 1980s. One thing we
    do know is that, in this leadership election, this one man did not make a difference.

CLEVERLY: But you're a car! You're not
              qualified.

KIT: I was created by a shadowy billionaire
              for a private police force operating
              under a PPP* contract without any
              proper government oversight.

STEWART: Okay, yeah, you're qualified. And you
              want to team up?

KIT: My logic circuits tell me that a
              compromise will serve us all.

CLEVERLY: Why us?

KIT: You were the first to open my door.

STEWART: I *told* you the cookies on the seat
              were a trap!

CLEVERLY: Daaamn.

KIT: I apologise. It was a necessary ruse.

———————————

[Upstairs. The same time]

RAAB: Are we really stronger
              together, though?

JAVID: Do you know what a
              triumvirate is, Dom?

RAAB: I went to Oxford, you know.

JAVID: I'll take that as a 'no' then. A
              triumvirate is when three powerful
              people work together for a common goal.
              Case in point: the Second Triumvirate
              dominated Roman politics. From its
              efforts the Roman Empire grew. We could
              do that too, Dom. You could be a modern
              Lepidus, Dom! A triumvir!

---

* Public-private partnerships seem to have been a financial model for privatising public
services without having to admit you were doing it. Our ancestors put a lot of effort into
finding ways to do this.

RAAB:	This Lepidus guy does sound pretty cool. A triumvirate? Okay, I'm in!
JAVID:	Good boy.
RAAB:	[Leaving] See you at the speeches.

HANCOCK:	Not going to tell him who the other triumvirs were?
JAVID:	Nope.
HANCOCK:	Why?
JAVID:	
HANCOCK:	Ah. We're stabbing, not shagging, aren't we?
JAVID:	Yup.

[A conference room. Some hours later]

LIDINGTON:	Phil! Wasn't expecting to see you at the leadership hustings.
HAMMOND:	Why not? I love this stuff.
LIDINGTON:	Really?
HAMMOND:	God, yes. It's like *Celebrity Big Brother* but with racist politicians.
LIDINGTON:	Isn't that just... *Celebrity Big Brother*?
HAMMOND:	True. And you?
LIDINGTON:	Leadership hustings are a guilty pleasure. I think it's because they remind me a lot of beer festivals.
HAMMOND:	I can see that. Lots of weird old men ticking things off lists...
LIDINGTON:	Fake hipsters using it as cover to be a bit racist...

HAMMOND: Speaking of: Dom's up!

RAAB: [At the podium] The Brexit talks
                disgraced our proud nation!

HAMMOND: [Shouting] *You led them, you
                little tit!*

LIDINGTON: Phil, don't heckle.

HAMMOND: I can't help it. It's like being
                lectured on trade law by a Moss
                Bros manager.

LIDINGTON: [Shouting] *Eulalie! Eulalie!*

HAMMOND: What are you doing?

LIDINGTON: Sorry. Just wanted to see if it
                would work.

HAMMOND: This is a pretty terrible speech.

LIDINGTON: Indeed. I was expecting Raab to knife
                Javid and Hancock at least, but he's
                being surprisingly conciliatory. It's
                making him look weak.

GOVE: [Ethereal voice] jAVid aND HaNCoCK aRE
                SaboTAGiNG hIS caMPAign.

HAMMOND: Fuck! Don't do that. Where are you?

GOVE: SoRRy. LisTENiNG iN frOM tHE CorRIDor
                wHIle i pREpARe. LeT Me sTArT aGAin.
                i WiLL mAke A 'cONNecTiNG' sOUnD.

HAMMOND:

LIDINGTON:

GOVE: boO BeEP.

LIDINGTON: McVey seems to be awfully obsessed
                 with daytime telly.

HAMMOND: Is Esther... is she feuding with
                 Lorraine Kelly?!*

LIDINGTON: TV presenters need to be taken down a
                 peg or two. I feel her pain.

HAMMOND: What?! Why?

[A party. The previous year]

LIDINGTON: [Shouting] The *duck* had the talent!

PHILLIP   [Throwing a chair] Fuck *you*,
SCHOFIELD: Lidington!

LIDINGTON: [Throwing a chair back] Get back in
                 your broom cupboard, you hack!

[The conference room. Again]

LIDINGTON: No reason.

HAMMOND: Who's next?

LIDINGTON: Hang on. I'll check the programme
                 notes. Okay, Matt Hancock is going to
                 talk to us about 'channelling a new
                 paradigm in people-engagement'.

HAMMOND: What does that mean? Is he trying
                 to be prime minister or sell us
                 healing magnets?

LIDINGTON: Don't blame me. I'm just reading what
                 it says here.

---

* The original transcript of this tape features a rare handwritten side note. For reasons
unknown, it simply says: 'The *role* of Lorraine Kelly.'

HANCOCK:	As you can see on my deck, I... yes, a hand up at the back?
HAMMOND:	What's a 'deck'?
HANCOCK:	[Pointing at the big screen] This is.
HAMMOND:	Your PowerPoint slides?
HANCOCK:	Yes, my deck.
HAMMOND:	You could just say PowerPoint slides.
HANCOCK:	Look, if we can move on...
HAMMOND:	With the PowerPoint slides?
HANCOCK:	Yes. With the *deck*.
LIDINGTON:	[Aside] Shhh, Phil. You shouldn't tease Matt.
HAMMOND:	Oh, *come on*. He deserves it. His PowerPoint—
LIDINGTON:	'Deck'.
HAMMOND:	His *fucking PowerPoint slides* are titled 'Uber, But For Politics'. Anyway, why are you suddenly on Team Matt?
LIDINGTON:	He gave out doggy bags. Here, look.
HAMMOND:	Oh *shit*! Chorizo corn!
LIDINGTON:	[Munching] Yup.

ANGRY MAN AT THE PODIUM:	[Shouting] Brexit means Brexit!
HAMMOND:	Which one is this again?
ANGRY MAN:	[Shouting louder] Brexit means Brexit!
LIDINGTON:	I don't recognise him. Mark Harper, maybe?
ANGRY MAN:	*Brexit means Brexit!*

ANNOUNCER:	Security to the podium please! Intruder in conference room three! Security!
HAMMOND:	Not Mark Harper, then.
LIDINGTON:	I'm still not ruling it out.

LIDINGTON:	Are we getting Rory today?
HAMMOND:	No, he's doing his announcement in a tent outside, I think.
LIDINGTON:	What?
HAMMOND:	Oh, don't ask me. I assume it's something millennials do, like... oh... what's that thing everyone under forty spends all their money on?
LIDINGTON:	Avocados?
HAMMOND:	Rent.

HAMMOND:	Anyway, shhh. I think Michael's up next.
GOVE:	yES. I aM juST leAViNG tHE GrEEn rOoM.
LIDINGTON:	Aren't you all in the corridor?
GOVE:	MaTT hANcocK haS tOLD mE It Is a RoOM aND iT iS GrEEn.
HAMMOND:	Of course he has.
GOVE:	I fIND tHIS CoNFuSING. iT aPPeaRs tO Be A CorrIDOR. iT LooKS bROWn aND...
LIDINGTON:	Focus, Michael.

LIDINGTON:	Is it me, or is Michael a bit... flat?

HAMMOND: I think... No. Ignore me.

LIDINGTON: What?

HAMMOND: It's just... Do you get the impression these days that he doesn't really *want* to destroy the world any more?

LIDINGTON: For an eldritch horror, he does spend a lot of time at village fetes.

GOVE: HoW WaS i?

LIDINGTON: Michael, please don't take this the wrong way, but are you *sure* you want this?

GOVE: i Am an eLDrITcH hORRor. i MUst sEEk pOWer. iT is WhY i ExIST.

HAMMOND:

GOVE: aLTHouGH I wiLL haVE to GiVE uP ramBLERs cLUb...

LIDINGTON:

GOVE: aND thE ViLLAge cOMMitTEE...

HAMMOND: [Gently] Michael...

GOVE: [Firmly] nO I... i deFINiTELy wANt ThIS!

GOVE: i WAs GoING to mAKe a VicTORIa sPOngE.

HAMMOND: What?

GOVE: For tHE ViLLagE FeTE. JeREmy GaVE mE sOMe lOVelLY JaM fOr iT. HoMEmaDE.

HAMMOND: I can't believe I'm saying this, but you do know that you don't *have* to consume the world, right?

GOVE: i aM aN eLDrITCh hORROr.

LIDINGTON: Don't let that define you.

GOVE: iT Is aLL I kNOw.

LIDINGTON: Is your heart really in this?

GOVE: I cANnoT fIGHt wHaT i AM.

HAMMOND: 'Who'.

GOVE: SoRRy?

LIDINGTON: You're a 'who' to us, not a 'what'.

GOVE: yOU aRe... tOo KiND. No I MuST. bUT...

LIDINGTON: Yes?

GOVE: gENtLEmEN, wHEn mY daRKNesS dESCenDS
              oN thIS pLAnE i WiLL fLAY youR
              mINDs laST.

HAMMOND: Erm... Thanks?

HAMMOND: Well, that was horrifying.

LIDINGTON: We staying for Boris?

HAMMOND: Nah. It only encourages him. He'll
              probably send Liz Truss in his place
              anyway. This is too close to being
              actual work.

LIDINGTON: Or Grayling. Or Francois.

HAMMOND: Johnson, Truss, Grayling and Francois.
              The Cabinet we don't want but
              definitely deserve.

LIDINGTON: What about Javid, Leadsom
              and the rest?

HAMMOND: It's all just blending into one now,
              to be honest. It's not like we've
              heard anyone provide a coherent plan.

LIDINGTON: Message from Theresa: 'Watching this in Wethers and getting shitfaced.'

HAMMOND: Okay, now *that* is a plan I can get behind. Let's go.

CHAPTER TWENTY-FIVE

A WHOLE NEW WORLD

In July 2019 Boris Johnson was elected leader of the Conservative Party. He immediately began to place his most loyal supporters in positions of power. For many long-serving Conservative MPs, the writing was now on the wall.

[Phil Hammond's new office. Westminster]

HAMMOND: [Watching Johnson on television] 'The guy ropes of self doubt?' Fuck me.

GOVE: [Outside his window] yES. iT wAS preTTy bAD.

HAMMOND: Jesus Christ, Michael. Why are you clinging to the wall? And why are you all... tentacles?

GOVE: ElDRitcH hORroR.

HAMMOND:

GOVE:

HAMMOND: ... And?

GOVE: sORRy. I feLT thAT anSWeReD bOTh qUEsTiONs. CaN i CLiMB iN?

HAMMOND: What?

GOVE: tHIs iS A neW oFFicE. YoU hAVE To ReINviTE mE.

HAMMOND: I thought that was vampires?

GOVE: nO. AnD plEASe cAN wE trY aND aVOId
           cULTuRal sTEReoTypEs.

HAMMOND: Sorry.

GOVE: iT's fiNe. i'M jUsT... IT's bEEn
           a LoNG daY.

HAMMOND: Why were you outside the window,
           anyway? And why so many... eyes?

GOVE: HaVE yOU bEEn outSIDe tODay, PhIL?

HAMMOND: Not since this morning.

GOVE: iT iS HoTTEr thaN tHE sUN oUTsIDe
           tODay. AnD sKInSUIts aREN't
           brEATHAble.

HAMMOND: Huh.

GOVE: tHErE iS a REAsoN CtHULhU woN'T TaKE
           ThE CeNtrAL LiNE. AnYWaY, I jUST
           waNTEd tO seE HoW ThE nEW oFFIcE wAS.

HAMMOND: It's... small. Backbenching again is
           weird. But at least I don't have to
           worry about Jesse Norman shitting on
           the carpet any more.

GOVE: i'M pRETTy ceRTAin tHAT wAS
           larRY thE CaT.[*]

HAMMOND: That's what Jesse said too.

           ───────────────

HAMMOND: So... if he asks, will you serve?

GOVE: i HAvE nO ChOIcE. ChaOS muST ReIGN.

HAMMOND: I think that's a given. What are you
           hoping for?

GOVE: TraNSPoRT.

---

[*] While the presence of a cat in Downing Street may seem normal to modern readers, it
is worth remembering that our ancestors were as yet unaware that cats had achieved a
higher level of consciousness than humans at least 10,000 years earlier. They just didn't
want the responsibility. The first cat to officially hold the title of prime minister would be
Smudge in 2784.

HAMMOND: Really?

GOVE: GoD, yES. ThE AmOUNT of humAN mISERy
             aND sUFfering oNE caN InfLICT wITH
             tHE DfT FraNCHiSE fraMEwork!

GOVE: AnYwAY, i MUsT dePArT. I jUSt wANtEd
             tO sEE hOW yOu wErE doInG.

HAMMOND: Thanks for popping in.

GOVE: I'LL usE tHE wINDOw aGAIn, if yoU
             DoN'T mIND.

HAMMOND: Go for it. Can you shut it after
             you leave? I've got a meeting in a
             minute and...

STEWART: [Outside the window] Afternoon!

HAMMOND: ... or don't. Because *of course* there
             are more people out there. Rory, we're
             three floors up. Why are you outside
             my window?

STEWART: Just off to put my resignation in.
             Quicker to move around this way.
             Want me to drop yours off at the
             same time?

HAMMOND: No. I did it yesterday.

STEWART: Righto. I'll be off, then. I see
             there's a queue!

HAMMOND: What?

DOMINIC   [Clinging to the wall] *Vive la*
GRIEVE: *résistance!*

HAMMOND: *Oh, come on.*

GRIEVE: It is I! Dominic Grieve! You are
             expecting me.

HAMMOND: Doesn't *anyone* use doors any more?!

192

GRIEVE: Johnson has eyes everywhere. We move
                in the shadows.

HAMMOND: You sent me an Outlook invite.

GRIEVE: I did not wish to be impolite.

HAMMOND: Then use the fucking door next time.

HAMMOND: What do you want, anyway?

GRIEVE: To complete your induction.

HAMMOND: Into what?

GRIEVE: The resistance!

HAMMOND: That's an actual thing?

GRIEVE: Yes. And we have a HR induction
                checklist for it.

HAMMOND: A checklist.

GRIEVE: Yes.

HAMMOND: Is 'How to scale Parliamentary
                offices' on it?

GRIEVE:

HAMMOND:

GRIEVE: Yes. The wall-climbing module is
                only short.

HAMMOND: No.

GRIEVE: We train you in pairs. David Gauke is
                out here, waiting for you!

DAVID GAUKE: [Faintly] Hello!

HAMMOND:

GRIEVE:

GAUKE: [Faintly] Can someone help? I think
                I'm stuck.

HAMMOND:

GRIEVE:	I'll... just tick you off as not needing the wall-climbing training for now.
HAMMOND:	Please do.
GAUKE:	[Faintly] Please. Anyone? I think I'm really in a bit of a spot here.
HAMMOND:	[Closing the window] Fucking hell.

\<Knocking at the door\>

HAMMOND:	Oh, thank God. Someone normal. Who is it?
WILLIAMSON:	It's me.
HAMMOND:	Oh, *fuck my life*. Not that chickenshit.
WILLIAMSON:	What did you say?!
HAMMOND:	I said... come in. Um... new Chief Whip?
WILLIAMSON:	Flattery will get you nowhere.
HAMMOND:	Really? You seem to be doing all right.
WILLIAMSON:	I will not dignify that with an answer.
HAMMOND:	Is it Chief Whip, then?
WILLIAMSON:	Maybe. I... we're talking. I was promised lots of things.
HAMMOND:	Ha! Righto. Let me know how that works out for you.
WILLIAMSON:	Anyway, I am not here to debate the new order with you.
HAMMOND:	What do you want then?
WILLIAMSON:	I am here with a warning. My sources tell me you flirt with the resistance...

HAMMOND: Sources.

WILLIAMSON: Yes.

HAMMOND: My Outlook calendar.

WILLIAMSON:

HAMMOND:

WILLIAMSON: Yes.

HAMMOND: Nice work, Bergerac.

WILLIAMSON: All I'm saying is that you should
              tread carefully, Hammond. I have not
              forgotten the wrongs you inflicted on
              me. I can be merciful, but—

LIDINGTON: Am I interrupting?

HAMMOND: Absolutely not. Come on in.

WILLIAMSON: Will you *please* take me seriously!
              The Leader demands absolute ob—

LIDINGTON: Did he just say leader with a
              capital letter?

HAMMOND: I think so.

WILLIAMSON: Do *not* mock me! Both of you beware!

HAMMOND: Of what? We're just backbenchers.

LIDINGTON: Torn bench cushions, maybe. They
              can pinch.

WILLIAMSON: *You will respect me!*

HAMMOND: Toddle along, little chicken farmer.

LIDINGTON: I thought he sold fireplaces?

HAMMOND: Ah yes. My mistake.

WILLIAMSON: *The Leader is watching!*

LIDINGTON: Capital 'L' again. How lovely.

[Door slams]

LIDINGTON:	What a frightful little man now.
HAMMOND:	Oh, he was always frightful. It was just easier to ignore him before. Anyway, don't worry. I still know where he keeps his Space Marines.
LIDINGTON:	The Ultragavines? Fascinating lore...
HAMMOND:	Don't start. What did you want, anyway?
LIDINGTON:	Theresa says she's in Wethers again. Want to go?
HAMMOND:	God, yes.

CHAPTER TWENTY-SIX

THERE IS ANOTHER...

As he cemented his control over the party, Boris Johnson invited Conservative MPs to a garden party at Downing Street. Few among the old guard were under any illusions about what this meant for their futures. Outside, Johnson talked to the press about his demand for complete loyalty from all.

———————————

[Downing Street. The garden]

HAMMOND: This the worst party I've been to in
             a long time. The food is bad, nobody
             wants to make eye contact, and everybody
             is trying to fuck everyone else.

LIDINGTON: Rees-Mogg seems to be enjoying it.

HAMMOND: Of course he is. It's exactly like
             public school.[*]

LIDINGTON: Why are we here again?

HAMMOND: Gauke wants us to scope out which way
             people will jump under the new regime.

LIDINGTON: Right. We should probably stay off
             the booze, then.

HAMMOND: Agreed.

WILLIAMSON: [Approaching] Gentlemen! The Leader
             welcomes you.

———

[*]   Curiously, our ancestors seem to have referred to private schooling as 'public'. This seems to have been another one of the many ways they tried to fool themselves that things were fairer than they actually were.

LIDINGTON: Is he capitalizing both the 'T' *and*
               the 'L' now?

HAMMOND: Waiter! Wine, please! Leave
               the bottle.

WILLIAMSON: Are you not impressed by his
               benevolence? See how The Leader is
               good to his friends.

LIDINGTON: You mean the sandwiches?

WILLIAMSON: Yes.

LIDINGTON:

WILLIAMSON: Witness the *vol au vents*!

HAMMOND:

WILLIAMSON: They're from Pret!

HAMMOND: Well, fuck me, hold the phones! I'll
               call Barnier and let him know you're
               serious now. [Sipping a drink] Mind
               you, I'll say this for Randolph,
               at least he's opened up the wine
               cellar for this.

WILLIAMSON: Stop calling The Leader that!

HAMMOND: Why? I thought he idolised Churchill?

WILLIAMSON: Not that one.

HAMMOND: Could have fooled me.

WILLIAMSON: Right now, The Leader is out there in
               front of Downing Street giving all you
               traitorous MPs a piece of his mind!

LIDINGTON: Right now?

WILLIAMSON: Yes!

LIDINGTON: Out there?

WILLIAMSON: Yes!

LIDINGTON: But we're all here in the garden,
                Gavin. Nobody is listening.

WILLIAMSON:

LIDINGTON:

WILLIAMSON: Shit.

HAMMOND: *Classic* Randolph.

WILLIAMSON: I find your constant lack of faith in
                The Leader disturbing.

LIDINGTON: You're Education Secretary, Gavin. Not
                Grand Moff Tarkin.

HAMMOND: Nice reference. Never pegged
                you as a fan.

LIDINGTON: John Williams* soundtrack.

HAMMOND: Ah.

WILLIAMSON: Are you two listening to me?!

LIDINGTON: Why didn't he give you Defence back,
                by the way?

WILLIAMSON: Um... We decided that it wasn't the
                best way for me to serve.

HAMMOND: Because of your tendency to butt-dial
                the Chinese?

WILLIAMSON: No! Because at Education I can shape
                the minds of the future.

HAMMOND: How? You've clearly never had one
                of your own.

LIDINGTON: I thought Defence was what you
                loved, though?

---

* Williams was one of several iconic, prolific composers active at the time. Indeed, modern
students of ancient cinema have long known that if an exam asks for the name of a
soundtrack's composer, the answer is invariably either 'John Williams' or 'Hans Zimmer'.

WILLIAMSON: I love what The Leader tells
                me to love.

HAMMOND: Well, that's a horrifying
                mental image.

WILLIAMSON: You know what I mean!

LIDINGTON: But Defence gave you a chance
                to play with those little Star
                Marines you like.

WILLIAMSON: Space Marines! The Ultragavines
                are Space Marines! How can you not
                understand this?! *Gah*...

[Gavin storms off]

HAMMOND: You knew they were Space Marines,
                didn't you?

LIDINGTON: Oh, yes. I've been reading his lore
                guide again. It's surprisingly well
                written. Don't tell him that, though.

GOVE: wAS tHAt GaVIn?

HAMMOND: Yes.

GOVE: hE LoOKeD aNGrY.

HAMMOND: We do try.

LIDINGTON: Should you be talking to us?

GOVE: nOT rEALLy. jOhNSOn wON't lIKE iT.

LIDINGTON: Is it strange having another horror
                in government?

GOVE: oH nO, joHNSoN's huMAN.

HAMMOND: Really?!

GOVE: yEs. aLL tHE trULY awFuL crEATuRes
                aRE. I aM No LoNGeR aLOnE iN thE
                gOVErNMeNT, thOUGh. ThERe iS aNOtHER.

LIDINGTON: *Return of the Jedi!*

HAMMOND: Well spotted.

GOVE: tHE dUcK.

LIDINGTON: Sorry, what?

GOVE: tHe DuCK iS bACk.

HAMMOND: Okay, I appreciate that we've had some very odd conversations over the years, but this is genuinely up there.

GOVE: dO yOU reMeMbER chRIs gRAyLInG's DuCK?

HAMMOND: I remember Chris not understanding CapEx vs OpEx.

LIDINGTON: Oh... wait... Margaret! The comfort duck!

GOVE: M'GrEH. UNDeAD hORRor. SoWEr oF ChAOs. ThE oNE wHO eATs ThE FleSH oF tHEIr oWN. iT WhiSPErS tO jOhNSOn, cONStANTlY.

HAMMOND: While I have been drinking more than usual lately, I feel like I would have noticed a duck following Boris Johnson around.

GOVE: m'GReH WeARs a SuIT.

HAMMOND: The beak would still be a clue.

GOVE: nO, a *skInSuIT!*

[Peels off skin]

GOVE: <Lich wail. Tenacles flail>

LIDINGTON: *Jesus Christ!*

HAMMOND: [Gagging] Oh, *nice one.* You've corked the wine. Thank you *very* much. *Waiter!*

GOVE: SoRRy, bUT dO yOU UNdeRstaND whAT I mEAn nOW?

HAMMOND: Yes, sadly.

LIDINGTON: Which one is M'Greh, then?

[Gove points]

DOMINIC   quACK
CUMMINGS:

HAMMOND: Christ.

LIDINGTON: Dominic Cummings is an eldritch duck?

GOVE: yES.

HAMMOND: Well, that explains a lot.

LIDINGTON: I suppose it must be nice to have
                some company, at least?

GOVE: I HaTE It.

HAMMOND: Why?

GOVE: M'GrEh iS evIL.

LIDINGTON: Um...

HAMMOND: And you're not?

GOVE: ceRTAInLY nOT. I muST iNFLicT PaIN,
                suFFERiNG aND chAOs on huMANIty. BuT
                aT LeASt i DOn'T blOG aBOut iT.[*]

LIDINGTON: It must be satisfying being in a
                Cabinet that actually revels in
                chaos, though?

GOVE: I sUPPoSe.

HAMMOND: You don't sound enthused.

GOVE: iT'S juST sO FoRCed. A coNSTAnt quEST
                for tHE 'oNE COoL trICk tO beAT
                paRLiameNT'.

HAMMOND: Ah.

---

[*] Our ancestors seem to have used blogs as a way of displaying their worst thoughts to others.
Historians are unsure why, but it is assumed that it had some kind of ritual significance.

GOVE: iT's gOVERnMEnt bY RedDIT thREad.[*]

GOVE: aNYwaY, i mUST gO. a PuPPy hAS
               jUsT arrived.

HAMMOND: Another attempt by Johnson to distract
               people? Cruel on the dog.

GOVE: dISTRacTion? iT's mY DiNnER.

LIDINGTON: Wait, what?

GOVE: iT's mY cThuBEr eATs oRDer.
               i'M staRVinG.

HAMMOND: Well, that's... horrifying.

GOVE: i mUSt gO. iT WiLL geT cOLd.

HAMMOND: Did you ever think we'd reach a point
               where the person who eats puppies
               was only... What..? The fifth most
               horrifying member of the government?

LIDINGTON: Not really. This is hardly our finest
               hour, is it?

HAMMOND: At least it can't get much worse.

STEPHEN: Gentlemen.

HAMMOND: Oh fuck *this*. I'm going to the bar.

STEPHEN: Phil! Come back! We can still be
               friends, can't we?!

LIDINGTON: Do you know what fascism *really*
               is, Stephen?

STEPHEN:

LIDINGTON: It's not men in silly hats with
               skulls on. That's just television.
               Fascism is small men accepting big
               jobs as a way of trying to justify
               doing terrible things.

[*] See previous footnote on blogs. Magnify worst thoughts by twelve.

STEPHEN:

LIDINGTON: Goodbye, Stephen. You've made
your choice. Make the most of it,
while it lasts.

CHAPTER TWENTY-SEVEN

PLANNING FOR THE FUTURE

In December 2019 Boris Johnson finally called a general election. His campaign team immediately sprang into action. The first order of the day was deciding exactly what they would be campaigning on...

[A bar in Westminster]

GRANT SHAPPS: Welcome to the first meeting of the campaign strategy group. Let's start by brainstorming for a bit. Remember, there are no bad ideas!

WILLIAMSON: Poster campaign in Games Workshop[*] branches!

GRAYLING: Blue rubber ducks!

SHAPPS: Okay, there are *some* bad ideas.

SHAPPS: We're not putting 'Vote Tory' posters in Games Workshop, Gavin.

WILLIAMSON: Why not?

SHAPPS: Because 'Teens who play *Warhammer*' is not a key demographic for us.

WILLIAMSON: *40K*.

SHAPPS: What?

WILLIAMSON: It's *Warhammer 40K*.

---

[*] The ritual significance of Games Workshop is something archaeologists are still trying to establish. A link with lead-modelling is clear, as evidenced by the number of offerings discovered during excavations throughout the south-east.

SHAPPS:	What's the differ—
MORDAUNT/ STEPHEN:	*Don't ask that!!*
SHAPPS:	Moving swiftly on, does anyone have any more realistic ideas?
MORDAUNT:	Are there any achievements we can focus on?
SHAPPS:	Penny, he's been prime minister for three months. You can't even worm a cat in that time.
MORDAUNT:	Yes, but *we've* been in power for nine years, so...
SHAPPS:	No, we haven't.
MORDAUNT:	What? We've been in power nine years!
SHAPPS:	We haven't.
MORDAUNT:	Yes, we have! First David Cameron—
SHAPPS:	Who?
MORDAUNT:	Then Theresa May—
SHAPPS:	Doesn't ring a bell...
MORDAUNT:	You were *there*, Grant!
SHAPPS:	No, I wasn't.
MORDAUNT:	
SHAPPS:	Three months. No time to do anything. It's all Labour's fault. We clear?
MORDAUNT:	You can't just deny that two previous Tory governments existed.
SHAPPS:	What governments?
MORDAUNT:	This is *insane!*
SHAPPS:	Penny, you're starting to sound like you don't believe in this project. Do I need to send for Priti Patel?

MORDAUNT: [Quickly] Three months it is.

SHAPPS: That's better.

STEPHEN: We could do the bus thing again?

SHAPPS: Bus thing?

STEPHEN: Big number on a red bus. Worked in
               the referendum.

SHAPPS: What numbers?

STEPHEN: Twenty thousand cops? Forty new
               hospitals? The Leader has thrown both
               of those around a lot lately.

MORDAUNT: Aren't those... um...

SHAPPS: ... bollocks?

STEPHEN: You mean unlike 'an extra three
               hundred and fifty million pounds
               for the NHS'?

SHAPPS: Okay, point taken.

SHAPPS: I'm prepared to concede that a bus
               might be a good idea. Any other ideas
               for what we could put on it, though?

MORDAUNT: Where's Michael? He's good at
               this stuff.

SHAPPS: He said he had another meeting.

[Deep under the South Pacific. The same time]

THE OLD ONES: LeT'S bEGIn bY LooKING aT laST yeAR's
              OBjECTivES And KPiS. FiRsT One:
              sOW ChaOS.

GOVE: SO i FEeL i'Ve dONe weLL heRE...

207

[In Westminster]

STEPHEN: Seriously, though. Why don't we just do the NHS bus thing again? It clearly worked and The Leader loved that last time.

SHAPPS: No, he didn't.

STEPHEN: Yes, he did.

SHAPPS: It was nothing to do with him.

STEPHEN: There are photos of him in *front* of the bus, Grant. Pointing at it.

SHAPPS: No there aren't.

STEPHEN: But...

MORDAUNT: [Sighing] Let it go, Stephen.

SHAPPS: I do think you're on the right track here, though. Is there a *different* EU slogan we could put on the bus?

HAMMOND: [Walking in] You could put 'One point three billion pounds a week knocked off the British economy' but it isn't really a vote winner.

STEPHEN: Phil!

SHAPPS: Hey! This is a private meeting!

WILLIAMSON: *Get out! Traitor!*

HAMMOND: Make me. This is a Commons bar. You're in an open area.

SHAPPS: [Grumbling] There were no free meeting rooms.

WILLIAMSON: Heretic! Begone! Let the wrath of The Leader descend on you, like fire from—

HAMMOND: Oh, grow up, Gavin. You're not an inquisitor — you just like painting them.

208

HAMMOND: Anyway, don't worry, I'm going. I just wanted to come over and remind Chris about Lidington's leaving drinks later.

STEPHEN: David's having...? I didn't see an email about them.

HAMMOND: He's keeping it small. Just friends and...

STEPHEN: Oh.

HAMMOND: Ah. I mean...

STEPHEN: It's okay. I understand.

HAMMOND: David probably just forgot to put you on the email.

STEPHEN: Huh? Oh. Oh yeah...

HAMMOND: If you wanted to pop in, I'm sure he wouldn't mind.

STEPHEN: Oh yeah. Thanks. Um... yeah. I mean, I would, but you know... I'm busy with this election stuff. You know how it is...

HAMMOND: I bet David didn't mean to forget you. He was a bit angry at you at first, but he's calmed down now.

STEPHEN: It's fine. No biggie.

HAMMOND: Sure?

STEPHEN: Yeah, I'll skip it. But tell him... I miss you.

HAMMOND: You miss *us*?

STEPHEN: *Him*. Say I *will* miss *him*.

WILLIAMSON: [Mumbling] David Lidington's a heretic too.

EVERYONE: Shut the *fuck* up, Gavin.

CHAPTER TWENTY-EIGHT

LAST ONE'S GONE

Like many of the Conservative 'Old Guard' (Phil Hammond included), David Lidington announced that he would be standing down at the December 2019 general election. Before saying goodbye to the House forever, though, a leaving party was called for...

———————

[A party]

HAMMOND: This place always looks so desperate.

LIDINGTON: I know what you mean.

HAMMOND: It's just old men, sitting alone at
              tables, mumbling racist nonsense to
              themselves.

LIDINGTON: Yes, well, unfortunately Wetherspoons
              wasn't taking bookings, so a Commons
              bar it is.

LIDINGTON: Of course, it's the people that
              matter, not the place.

HAMMOND: That's true. And you've certainly had
              a good turnout tonight.

LIDINGTON: Yes, I'm rather touched.

HAMMOND: Even Rory's here.

LIDINGTON: He is? Where?

STEWART: [Clinging to the wall outside]
              Wouldn't miss it!

HAMMOND: No sign of Skeletor and his
                minions yet?

MORDAUNT: [Arriving] Actually, I bumped
                into Gavin on the way in. He was
                lurking outside.

LIDINGTON: Penny! How lovely to see you.

MORDAUNT: I growled at him, and he scurried off.

HAMMOND: I suspect it's only a
                temporary reprieve.

LIDINGTON: But a beautiful, if temporary, present
                nonetheless. Thank you.

MORDAUNT: My pleasure.

HAMMOND: I hear you've been knifed now?

MORDAUNT: Oh yes. I knew it was coming.

LIDINGTON: Too qualified? Too female? Or too much
                of a threat?

MORDAUNT: To be honest, with this lot they're
                all the same thing. But enough about
                me. This is your night. And this is
                quite the party you've got going on.
                Is Ken Clarke around?

HAMMOND: In the corner by the *Mortal Kombat*
                machine. Last time I was over there,
                he was ripping Liam Fox's spine out.

MORDAUNT: In game?

HAMMOND: Sure. Let's go with that.

GOVE: hELLo DaVId.

LIDINGTON: Michael! You made it! What a
                pleasant surprise.

GOVE: aS If I'D mISs tHIs. i eVEn bROUghT
                sOmE sNACks fOR thE buFFeT.

211

MORDAUNT: Um...

LIDINGTON: That's very generous of you but...

GOVE: CuPCaKEs. i mADe theM MySElf.

LIDINGTON: [Quietly] Oh, thank God.

_____

LIDINGTON: I really am touched by how many
               people are here.

HAMMOND: No sign of Stephen. I did tell him
               you probably wouldn't object.

LIDINGTON: I wouldn't, now I've calmed down a
               bit. But... well. At the same time, I
               do feel that he made his bed and must
               lie in it.

HAMMOND: Sorry, I shouldn't have bought it up.

LIDINGTON: It's fine.

HAMMOND: Wait, this'll cheer you up. *Grayling.*
               Grayling. Grayling.

GRAYLING: <Schplop> Hello!

LIDINGTON: Chris!

HAMMOND: How have you been, Chris?

GRAYLING: Oh, you know. Same old, same old.
               What's this, then?

LIDINGTON: My leaving party.

HAMMOND: [Aside] Can someone pass me a
               cupcake? Thanks.

GRAYLING: You're leaving?

HAMMOND: [Munching] We all are, Chris.

GRAYLING: You too?

HAMMOND: Yup.

GRAYLING: Blimey.

LIDINGTON: Theresa's gone too. She's not prime
minister any more, Chris.

GRAYLING: She isn't?!

HAMMOND: [Munching] No, Chris. She isn't.

GRAYLING: Gosh. How sad. I had no idea. Am I
leaving too?

HAMMOND: [Munching] Probably.

GOVE: aCtUAlly, nO. We'RE mAKiNG hIM hEAd
of The iNTElliGEnCE ComMItEE.[*]

GRAYLING: Oh, that sounds jolly fun! I'll...
Phil, are you alright?

LIDINGTON: I think he's choking. Hang on, I'll
do the Heimlich.

GRAYLING: Is he going to be okay? Is there
anything I can do?

LIDINGTON: It's fine, Chris. Go... go try the
buffet or something.

GRAYLING: [Wandering off] Righto.

LIDINGTON: He's coming round. Phil, can you—

HAMMOND: *The fucking Intelligence Committee?!*

GOVE: yES.

HAMMOND: How?! Why?! How does Chris keep
getting jobs?!

GOVE: fUnnILY eNOUgH, I aCTuALLy kNOw thE
aNSweR to ThIS oNE.

LIDINGTON: You do?

GOVE: yEs. LaST TiME I waS BeLOW, I dID
sOMe diGGIng. IT TuRNs oUT ChRIS
gRAyLInG iS aCTuaLLY a GoD.

---

[*] Records suggest that Chris Grayling was never, in fact, appointed to the Intelligence Committee. His candidacy was spiked by a challenge he didn't see coming.

HAMMOND:	What?
GOVE:	krAiLos. ThE GreEK gOD Of fAILinG uPWaRD.*
LIDINGTON:	Chris Grayling is... an ancient Greek god?
GOVE:	yEs. INCReDIBly pOWeRFuL, apPARenTLY.
HAMMOND:	Chris Grayling. The man standing over there by the buffet, who... wait for it... yup. The man who just poked himself in the eye trying to eat a cheese-and-pineapple cocktail stick.
GOVE:	I sAID pOWErFuL, nOT clEVer.
LIDINGTON:	Does he know?
GOVE:	sOMEtIMes. aPPaRENTly hE ForGEts.
HAMMOND:	Shouldn't he be where... I don't know, wherever gods live or something?
LIDINGTON:	He's just squirted ketchup on himself.
GOVE:	thEY'rE haPPIeR wiTh HIm doWN heRE.
HAMMOND:	I can't imagine why.
MAY:	[Entering] Who are we talking about?
LIDINGTON:	Theresa!
HAMMOND:	Chris Grayling. Apparently he's like Tom Bombadil, but shit.
LIDINGTON:	Isn't that just Tom Bombadil?
MAY:	I'm not even going to ask.
LIDINGTON:	Probably wise.
MAY:	That's reminded me, actually — whatever happened to Chris's comfort duck?
HAMMOND:	You *definitely* don't want to know the answer to that one. Trust me.

---

* While eldritch horrors have long been a feature of government, Chris Grayling remains the only Greek god to have so far played an official role in British politics.

[Some time later]

LIDINGTON: Thank you for coming, Theresa. I was worried you wouldn't make it.

MAY: I wouldn't miss this for the world! Sorry I was so late. I was busy preparing a smooth transition.

LIDINGTON: It's fine. I understand. Indeed, I'm impressed you're taking the high ground on that.

[The flat above Downing Street. That morning]

DECORATOR: Pleather?!

MAY: Yes. Everywhere. Black pleather sofas. Black pleather walls. Black pleather cabinet fronts. And paint the glass in the windows black. Can you make the ceiling look sticky, too? It needs to look sticky.

DECORATOR: But...

MAY: Just do it. And I want ultraviolet lights pointed at *everything*. Let's make sure he's in his comfort zone.

[The party]

MAY: Hmmm? The high ground? Yes... I've been taking that. Definitely.

HAMMOND: Oh yes, very 'high ground'.

MAY: [Innocently] What? I don't know what you mean.

HAMMOND: You're forgetting who signed
                off your final Downing Street
                decorating budget.

MAY: I just decided it was time to do some
                renovations, is all.

HAMMOND: Sure. I suppose the timing is just—

SHAILESH   Sorry to interrupt, but I've got to
VARA: go and I just wanted to pop over and
                say goodbye to David, and also to
                you, Theresa.

LIDINGTON: Oh, that's very kind of you!

VARA: I know we've all had our differences
                in the past.

MAY: We have? I mean... we have.

VARA: But I've always felt that on a
                personal level we got on.

LIDINGTON: We did? I mean... we did.

VARA: So, I wanted to say: it has been
                a pleasure serving in the Commons
                alongside you both.

[Vara departs]

HAMMOND: Okay, is one of you going to tell me
                who that actually was?

LIDINGTON: It's Shailesh.

MAY: Who?

LIDINGTON: You know... Shailesh. Shailesh Vara.

MAY: David, I was up until four in the
                morning cutting holes into the toilet
                cubicle walls in Number Ten. My brain
                is broken, and I have not yet had a
                drink. Who *is* that?

LIDINGTON: Damn. I was just reading off his
                badge. I was hoping you knew. Shall I
                look him up?

MAY: Nah. Whoever he was... it doesn't matter now. Anyway, I see Gavin has finally turned up. Shall I begin discreetly rounding up a Wetherspoons advance party? If I stay, I'll only end up ripping his face off.

LIDINGTON: Probably wise. I'm no longer paid to hold you back.

HAMMOND: And I wouldn't have held you back before.

MAY: I'll go grab Penny and Ken. See you in a bit.

WILLIAMSON: [Approaching] Gentlemen. I bring a message from The Leader.

HAMMOND: 'A wild Rattata appears!'

LIDINGTON: Gavin, why are you wearing a hooded cloak?

WILLIAMSON: It makes me look menacing.

HAMMOND: No, it makes you look like you got trapped in a duvet cover.

WILLIAMSON: It does not!

LIDINGTON: It absolutely does.

HAMMOND: Hang on... that *is* a duvet cover! You've just turned it inside out.

WILLIAMSON: It is not!

HAMMOND: Gavin, I can see the pattern.

LIDINGTON: Oh! So it is. Chibi Thatchers. How... um... lovely.

HAMMOND: Wait, Penny said she scared you off...

WILLIAMSON: If you will let me *finish*...

HAMMOND: I'm thinking you ran to your office,
               hid there until you got your courage
               back up, then grabbed the first thing
               you could find...

WILLIAMSON: Will you *listen* to me! I said I bring
               a message from The Leader.

LIDINGTON: [Gently] Gavin, are you wearing a
               duvet cover because you're worried
               Penny might see you again?

WILLIAMSON: *That's a lie!* I am The Leader's right
               hand. I *demand* you respect me!

LIDINGTON: Respect isn't something you demand,
               Gavin. It's something you earn.

HAMMOND: Plus, I don't want to even *think* about
               what that man does with his right hand.

WILLIAMSON: I am the power behind the throne! I
               am the terror that stalks the Commons
               in his name!

LIDINGTON: In a Chibi Thatcher duvet cover?

WILLIAMSON: [Shouting] *It's a cloak!* You mock me
               because you want to be me.

LIDINGTON: I can very much assure you that
               isn't the case.

WILLIAMSON: The Leader... he acknowledges my
               brilliance. He looks at me and sees
               the Primarch within.

HAMMOND: Gavin, waging war with plastic figures
               doesn't make you Napoleon.

WILLIAMSON: Lead!

HAMMOND: What?

WILLIAMSON: The plastic ones are for newbs and
               snowflakes. I only play with lead.

LIDINGTON: Well, that explains an awful lot.

                            218

WILLIAMSON: Anyway, *none of this matters*. I'm here
              because I have convinced The Leader
              to give you one more chance.

LIDINGTON: A chance at what?

WILLIAMSON: A chance at *redemption*. A chance to
              join our glorious crusade.

LIDINGTON: Oh God, not this again.

WILLIAMSON: Swear fealty gentlemen, here and
              now, and all will be forgotten. Like
              me, you will walk these halls with
              unchallenged authority and power,
              fearing nothing and—

HAMMOND: Gavin...

WILLIAMSON: What?

HAMMOND: I think Penny's coming over.

WILLIAMSON: [Quickly]
              AnywayThinkAboutItIMustGoNowBye!

LIDINGTON: That man is honestly one of the most
              awful people I've ever met.

HAMMOND: Agreed. Oh well. Wethers? Theresa
              is waiting.

LIDINGTON: Yes. But first... there's one thing
              I've always wanted to do.

HAMMOND: What's that?

LIDINGTON: Philip, would you care to join me
              in Gavin Williamson's office? I
              would like to stamp on his Space
              Marines, before they revoke our
              security passes.

HAMMOND:

LIDINGTON:

HAMMOND: David, this could be the beginning of
a *beautiful* friendship...[*]

---

[*] And it was.

PART TWO
THE SONGS OF BREXIT

LET IT GOVE

Sung to the tune of 'Let It Go' from Frozen

ThE sNOw gLOwS WhITe oVeR WhitEHall toNIGht,
nOT a sTAteSMan tO Be seEn.
UnITEd KinGDom ISolatED,
a PM wHo THInks sHe's a QUEen.
BaCK bENchES hOWliNg liKE THis snOWstORm nOW oUTsidE,
COuldN'T keEP it IN,
HEaveN knoWS I've trIEd.

DOn't LEt thEM in, DOn't let THem sEE,
Be tHE HorROR, yoU alwAYs haVE to BE!
ConCEal, dON't feEL, Don't let THEm knOW...

WeLL, NOw thEY KNow...

I AM GoVE! I am GOve!
CAn't hoLD it bAck ANY moRe.
I am GovE! I am goVe!
SHed thIS skiN aND taKE the floOR!
i DOn't cAre whAT tHEy're GOinG tO sAY!
Let THis stORm raGE oN.

EldriTCH cOld nEvEr bOtherEd mE anyWAy.

IT's fuNNY hOw sOmE diSTancE
mAkeS evEryTHing sEEm SMall.
FEArs of BoJO thAt cONtroLLed mE
cAn't gET tO mE at aLL!
It's TImE to sEE whAT I cAN do.
TESt hUManity's limITS aNd brEAk thrOUgh.
No RIght, NO wroNG, no RULes fOr mE...

<Eldritch scream>

I AM GoVE! I am GOve!
For PM I'll nOw TRy!
I am GovE! I am goVe!

<Banshee wail towards the sky>

HERe I sTAnd! And HErE I sTay!
LEt mY stORm rAge oN...

My TENtacleS sPReaD acrOSS WhitEHall's frOZen grOUnd,
mY SOul is SPirallinG iN dARkenED frACtals aLL arOUnd,
AnD onE tHOUght crystallisES liKE aN ICy blAst:
I'm nEvEr gOINg baCK! thE pASt is iN thE pASt!

i Am GoVe! I'm THE GOVE!
GoNNa risE like aN ELDer gOD!
i'M tHE GoVE! I'm The GOve!
mAY's eLDRitch PAwn iS GOne!

HeRE I STAnd! In thE ligHT oF daY!
LeT my STOrm rAge oN!

EldriTCH cOld nEvEr bOtherEd mE anywAY.

BE PREPARED

Sung to the tune of 'Be Prepared' from The Lion King

REES-MOGG:
I never thought the Baby Boomers essential.
They're crude, and unspeakably plain.
But maybe they've a glimmer of potential,
if allied to my vision and brain.

I can tell from the *Mail*'s comment section,
that of immigrants you're terrified.
But afeared as you are, pay attention!
Let's say it's about 'national pride'.

It's clear from your voting intentions,
that to Farage you were all running scared.
But we're talking EU secession!
Don't let the Remoaners catch you unawares!

So prepare for the chance of your lifetimes!
Be prepared for sensational news!
A shiny new era, is tiptoeing nearer...

BOOMER 1:
And where do we feature?

REES-MOGG:
Just listen to teacher!

I know it sounds sordid, but you'll be rewarded,
When at least I am given my dues!

For a Brexit as hard as we care...

Be prepared!

BOOMER 2:
Yeah! We'll be prepared!

BOOMER 3:
For what?!

REES-MOGG:
For the fall of the prime minister!

BOOMER 3:
Why, did she trip?

REES-MOGG:
No, you fools. We're going to overthrow her!

BOOMER 1:
Yeah! Great idea!

BOOMER 2:
Who needs a prime minister?!

BOOMERS [TOGETHER]:
No PM! No PM! La la la la laa la!

REES-MOGG:
Idiots!

There will be a PM!
I will be PM!
Stick with me, and the NHS will get more money again!

BOOMERS [TOGETHER]:
Yay! Long live the PM! Long live the PM! Ha ha!

It's great that we'll soon be protected!
From Polish families living next door.

REES-MOGG:
Of course, quid pro quo, you'll accept that,
I must move my own business offshore.
The future is littered with prizes,
and though I'm the main addressee.
The point that I must emphasise is...

You won't get Brexit without me!

So prepare for the coup of the century!
Be prepared for the murkiest scam!

Meticulous planning and Russian news spamming,
decades of denial,
is simply why I'll be,
PM undisputed!
Respected! Saluted!
And seen for the wonder I am.

Yes, my teeth and ambitions are bared!

Be prepared...

CAN YOU FEEL THE LOVE TONIGHT?

Sung to the tune of 'Can You Feel the Love Tonight?'
from The Lion King

McDONNELL:
I can see what's happening!

STARMER:
What?

McDONNELL
And they don't have a clue!

STARMER:
Who?

McDONNELL:
They'll pass their bill and here's the bottom line:
the north will go true blue!

STARMER:
Oh.

McDONNELL:
The lure of cross-bench action,
cooperation everywhere.
And in this new pragmatic atmosphere...
Disaster's in the air.

COOPER:
Can we kill no deal tonight?!
The peace of mind it brings.
The House for once in perfect harmony.
Except the Brexit wing.

BOLES:
We'll find a way to show her.
The PM has to know.
To crash out hard?! Impossible!
No deal just has to go.

COOPER
She's holding back, delaying.
For what? We can't decide.
If she were the PM that she thinks she is,
she wouldn't let this last chance slide!

BOLES/COOPER:
Can we kill no deal tonight?
The peace of mind it brings.
The House for once in perfect harmony.
Except the Brexit wing.
Can we kill no deal tonight?
The voting maths is hard.
Steer this through the night's uncertainties,
and that is where we are.

McDONNELL:
And if the bill passes tonight,
it can be assumed...

STARMER:
Indecisive days for us are history.

STARMER/McDONNELL:
In short, our Jez is doomed.

THE REES-MOGG SONG

Sung to the tune of 'Gaston' from Beauty and the Beast

CHOPE:
Gosh, it disturbs me to see you, Rees-Mogg,
looking so down and confused.
Every guy here'd love to be you, Rees-Mogg.
Even when failing your coup.

There's no Brexiteer as admired as you.
The *Daily Mail*'s favourite guy.
The ERG's awed and inspired by you.
And it's not very hard to see why...

No one's slick as Rees-Mogg!
Latin quips like Rees-Mogg!
Has opinions antagonistic as Rees-Mogg!

For there's no man in town half as manly.
The perfect Tory paragon!
You can ask any Raab, Chope or nanny...
and they'll tell you whose team they prefer to be on!

No one... off...
shores like Rees-Mogg!
Hates the poor like Rees-Mogg!
Thinks he's more than the sum of his parts like Rees-Mogg!

REES-MOGG:
As a statesmen, oh yes, I'm intimidating!

THE ERG [TOGETHER]:
My, what a guy, that Rees-Mogg.

REES-MOGG:
I needed encouragement.
Thank you, Chris Chope.

CHOPE:
Well, there's no one as easy to bolster, I hope!

Too much?

REES-MOGG:
Yep.

CHOPE:
No one spites like Rees-Mogg!
Talks 'men's rights' like Rees-Mogg!
Drags their party as far to the right as Rees-Mogg!

REES-MOGG:
When I write down my views in a paper,
my fellow MPs say a prayer.
First, I carefully aim for the boomers,
and I tell them white lies.

CHOPE:
Is that fair?

REES-MOGG:
I don't care.

CHOPE:
No one...
spouts like Rees-Mogg!
'Whatabouts' like Rees-Mogg!
Believes class as important as smarts as Rees-Mogg!

REES-MOGG:
I'm especially good when I'm Etonsplaining...

CHOPE:
Say it in Latin, Rees-Mogg!

REES-MOGG:
When I was a lad I read Kipling each day,
dreamed of empires British and large,

and now that I'm grown, my views still haven't changed,
that's why I push Brexit so hard...

CHOPE:
Who has brains like Rees-Mogg?
Can mansplain like Rees-Mogg!

REES-MOGG [INTERRUPTING]:
Dreams of succeeding Theresa May like Rees-Mogg.
I use hatchets in all of my decorating!

CHOPE:
Say it again!
Who's a man among men?
Who's the super-success?
Don't you know, can't you guess?!
Ask his fans and racist hangers-on!

There's one name in the House that the hard right espouse...

And that name's:
R E S...
R E S M O...
I believe there's another E...
It just occurred to me that I'm illiterate...
And I've never actually had to spell it out loud before...

REES-MOGG!

BE OUR GUEST

Sung to the tune of 'Be Our Guest' from
Beauty and the Beast

BARNIER:
Ma chérie, it is with deepest pride and greatest pleasure that
we welcome you back. And now we invite you to relax, let us
pull up a chair, as the EU Commission proudly considers...

... reopening your deal.

Be.
Our.
Guest.
Be our guest.
Put our resolve to the test.
Tie that noose around your neck, Thérèse!
Let history do the rest.

Open up
the talks again,
though you still don't have a plan.
Our negotiators here are vicious.
Don't believe? Ask Varoufakis!

You can sing,
you can dance,
but your problem is not France.
Gibraltan sovereignty is something Spain will test!
Go on, recite your red lines,
'Spite the looming deadline.

Be our guest!
Oui, our guest!
Be our guest!

Dom'nic Raab,
Steve Barclay,
Dave Davis back in the day.
All full of air, and bad hair,
a real gammon cabaret!

You're alone.
And you're scared.
But this deal was all prepared!
You weren't gloomy or complaining,
when first we were negotiating.

It's a joke.
It's a trick.
For this backstop you did pick!
Reopen this and one thing you can bet:

We'll see your lack of class,
and give you no free pass.

But be our guest!
(If you're stressed,
it's resigning we suggest.)
Be our guest!
Be our guest!
Be our guest!

Life is so unnerving,
for a PM who's not serving.
A smooth ship that they can whip, rely upon.
Ah, those good old days with a majority.
Sadly those good old days are now long gone!

Two whole years we've been waiting!
Needing more than obviating.
Needing excise, customs, rules on labour skilled.
Most days we just read the news all baffled.

Impractical and hazy,
your new bill is still just crazy!

DONALD TUSK:
Be our guest!
Be our guest!
Sakes alive, we'll all be blessed!
When deal's secured and thank the Lord,
this whole shitshow's put to rest.

No deal's bad.
She must see.
It hurts Britain more than we.
And while the ERG are mewling,
a disaster big is brewing.
'Brexit means
Brexit', fine,
but that's just a weaselly line.
It's not a plan and we are highly unimpressed!

There's way too much to do
in just a month or two!

But be our guest.

EU COMMISSION [TOGETHER]:
She's our guest!
She's our guest!
She's our guest!
Be our guest!
Be our guest!
Our command is your request.
It's two years since we had anybody here
who with brains was blessed.

Bring a deal,
not legalese.
And indeed, we'll aim to please.
While the time that's left is going,
let us help you,
we'll keep going...

BARNIER:
Clause by clause.
One by one.
'Til you shout, 'Enough, I'm done!'
As the truth of what you're doing manifests:
place party unity
above your country's need.
No, be our guest!
Be our guest!

Please, be our guest.

A Note on the Author

John Bull is a British journalist and historian. In his writing – for the *Guardian*, *Cult TV Times* and *The Dark Side*, among others – he explores how obscure and unexpected moments can change history. *The Brexit Tapes*, a satirical 'what-if?' alt-history of Brexit, is his first book.

@garius

Unbound is the world's first crowdfunding publisher, established in 2011.

We believe that wonderful things can happen when you clear a path for people who share a passion. That's why we've built a platform that brings together readers and authors to crowdfund books they believe in – and give fresh ideas that don't fit the traditional mould the chance they deserve.

This book is in your hands because readers made it possible. Everyone who pledged their support is listed below. Join them by visiting unbound.com and supporting a book today.

Richard Abraham
P. Justus Ackermann
Alexandre Adler
AJS
Matthew Alden-
    Farrow
Mark Alexander
Verity Allan
Ashley Allen
Andrew Anderson
Keith Anderson
Rod Anderson
Chris Andrews
Ian Andrews
Rosy Ansell
John Anstey
JK Arazi
Tiffany Arnold
Ghastly Artificer
Angela Ashby
Arshaad Asruf
MariaGabriella
    Atzori

David Austin
Nicholas 'Aquarion'
    Avenell
Andrew Aylett
James Aylett
Byron Aytoun
Jacquie B
Ollie B
Stephanie Baclin
James Baggaley
Caz Bailey
William Bailey
Richard Bairwell
Dave Baker
Rebecca Baldry
Phil Ball
Mountain Barber
Oliver Barker
Nick Barrass
Dan Barrett
Helen Bartlett
Simon Baskerville
Yves Bastide

Kate Baucherel
Zoony P Bear
Bob Beaupre
Marion Beet
    (Knitronomicon)
Garret Beggan
Peter Belk
Gavin Bell
Mike Bell
Daniel Bellamy
Ben
Patrick Bennett
Phillip Bennett-
    Richards
David Benson
Alex Benyon
Ben Best
Andreas Biermann
JJ Bill
Elizabeth Billington
Edward Bilson
Peter Binnersley
Simon Bisson

Jonathan Blanchard Smith
Graham Blenkin
Redundant Bloke
Arthur Blue
Michael Bolitho
Stephen Bonner
Ozaru Books
Lorna Booth
Lisa Bose
Sally Bosley
Huw Bowen
Paul Bowsher
Peter Bowyer
Aisling Boyle
Pete Bradshaw
Christian Brahms
Ben Brandwood
Steven Bray
Janet Brayshaw
Peggy Brett
Rich Bridgmount
Will Briggs
Jon Bright
David Brignall
Margaret Brinkley
Paul Brione
Nicholas Brooks
Ian Brown
Brian Browne
Dan Browne
Helen Browne
David Brownlee
Sam Bruce
Helen Bryant
Peter Bullen
Sally Bulmer
Huw Burford-Taylor

Oliver Burke
Alan Burkitt-Gray
Kathryn Busby
Morris Butler
Darryl Byrne
Matthew Byrne
Simon Callan
Helen Calvert
Chris Camp
Alexander Campbell
Crysta Campbell
Lore Campbell
Alistair Canlin
Thomas Canning
Kirsty Carpenter
Chris 'The Cake Runner' Carr
Ann Carrier
Henry Carruthers
Emma Carver
Nora Casey
Joseph Castle
Adam Catney
Lucy Cavell
Sally Cawdery
Elaine Chadwick
Jon Chadwick
Nadine Chahine
Peter Chalmers
Paul Chaplin
James Chapman
Kate Chapman
Ruth Chapple
KJ Charles
Philippa Charles
Lisa Charlesworth
Elizabeth Charlton
Rachel Chilton

Jonathan Chin
Chris and Sandra
Laura Churcher
Carl Clare
Claire Clark
Douglas Clark
John Clark
Nicola Clarke
Thomas Clarke
Ian Clay
Paula Claytonsmith
Stuart Clear
David Clements
Joanne Clements
Jim Clokey
Freyalyn Close-Hainsworth
Claire Coady
Paul Cocks
Genevieve Cogman
Oliver Cole
Clair Colgan
Robert Collier
Gill Collingwood
Brian Collins
Murray Colpman
John Concagh
Rachel Cook
Sam Cook
Lee Coomber
Brian Cooper
Sharon Corbet
Nick Corlett
Andrew Correia
Anne Costigan
Conrad Cotton-Barratt
Lorna Coupland

Ben Cowdell
Anne Cowley
Emma Cowley
Barbara Cox
David Cox
Hanne Craven-
    Carter
Ruth Crawford
Tom Cronin
Deborah Crook
Dave Cross
JP Cross
Sebastien Cross
Matthew Crowley
Alice Cruickshank
Karl Cubbon
Tony Cullen
Lynn Cullimore
Kristofer Cullum-
    Fernandez
Alexander Cunliffe
Ben Curthoys
Stuart Cuthbertson
Joshua Cutting
Anne D. (cheyinka)
Eleanor D'Acquitane
Greg D'Arcy
Pádraig D'Arcy
Victoria
    Daborn Tedder
Deirdre Daly
Jonathan Daniel
Steve Darcy
Vivek Das
    Mohapatra
Peter Davey
Chris Davie
Andrew Davies

G Davies
Neil Davies
E R Andrew Davis
David Dawson
Pierce De Courcy
Jasmin De Freitas
Saul P de Meldde
Alison Deane
Claire Debenham
Jack Deeth
Jennifer Delaney
Jamie Dempster
Mark Dennehy
Thomas Depierre
Ian Derbyshire
Patrick Dersjant
Martyn Dewar
John Dexter
Alex Dhawan
Pedro Dias
Miranda Dickinson
Jeanne Dietrick
Zeynep Dilli
Mike Dimmick
Rachel Dixon
Benedict Docherty
Alastair Dodd
Steve Dodd
J Doe
Noel Dolphin
Abigail Dombey
Sam Dooley
Paul Douglas
Oksana Dovorecka
John Dow
Joel Down
David Downing
Ken Doyle

Todd Drake
Neil Drayton
Peter Duffy
Liz Duggan
Chris Duncalf
Duncan
Sharon Dunford
Sophie Duport
Peter Durbin
Eleanor Durrant
Paul Duxbury
Susie Dye
Steven Dyer
Sam Easterby-Smith
Nick Eden
Sue Edgar
Lyn Edmonds
Jonny Edwards
Rebecca Edwards
Suzanne Edwards
Teresa Edwards
Nick Efford
Matthias Eiriksson
Ian Elders
Simon Elkins
John Elliott
Brad Emerson
Carrie Emery
Ed Emmott
Christopher
    Engelhard
Clare England
Martin English
M Etherton
Jude Evans
Keith Evans
Sarah Evans
Anthony Evershed

Jonathan Ewer
Robert Ewing
Jen Excell
Harley Faggetter
Rob Fahey
Chloe Fairbairns
Matt Farr
Rosie Fean
Thomas Fehmel
James Fenlon
Alex Ferguson
David Field
Benjamin Fisher
Alan Fleming
Roger Ford
James Forrester
Matthew Forrester
Nick Forster
Tom Foskett
David Fowkes
Jon Frame
Chris Francis
Will Frank
D Franklin
Dr A Franklin
Pete Franklin
Joanna Franks
Stuart Fraser
Thomas Freeman
Harry French
Mark Friswell
Andrew Fuller
Sarah G
Richard Gadsden
Colin Gallagher
Max Gallien
Paddy Galvin
Jayne Gamble

David John Gardner
Lyndsey Garrett
William Garrood
J. J. Gass
Tom Gauterin
Abigail Gawith
Sam Gawith
Rav Geoffry Cohen
Pete Gettins
Carlo Giannone
James Gibbons
Andy Gibson
Grant Gibson
Ian Gilbert
Adam Gilbride
Julie Giles
Bill Gillingham
David Gladman
Jon Glahome
Martin Gleadow
Martin Glew
Thomas Glithero
Jacob Gloor
Tara Glover
Tom Glover
Oliver Godby
Tim Godden
Nikola Goger
Eleanor Goldsmith
Celso Gomes
Katie Goodall
Julien Goodwin
Annette Goosey
Margaret Gordon
Michael Gordon
Tim Gordon
Rory Gormley
Ros Gough

Tom Grace
Carola Graf
Elaine Graham-
    Leigh
Ian Grant
Stefan Graunke
Sean Gray
Felipe Grazziotin
Arthur Green
Chris Green
Lilian Greenwood
Margaret Greenwood
Simon and Catherine
    Greenwood
Sophia Grene
Michael Griffin
Peter Griffith
Iain Griffiths
Julie Groom
James Gross
Chris Gurney
David Habbershaw
David Hagar
Susanna Hagelin
Tom Haines
Cris Hale
Graham Haley
Sally Hall
Howard Halliday
Dave Hallwood
Nik & Sarah Halton
Markus Hamel
Charlene Hamid
Yasmine Hamid
Russell Hammant
James Handscombe
Tim Hardy
Nicholas Harmer

Mel Harper
Simon Harper
David Harris
Jackie Harris
Greg Harrop
Victoria Hart
Theresa Harwood
Tim Harwood
Melinda Haunton
Patrick Haveron
Maximilian Hawker
Peter Hawkins
Stevy Haworth
Malcolm Hay
Graham Hayes
Katy Heaney
Cis Heaviside
Emma Heggie
Hans-Christian
    Heinz
Zandy Hemsley
Tristan Henderson
Benjamin Hendy
Sir Peter Hendy
Tracey Henley
Fritha Hennessy
Conrad Henson
James Hetherington
James Hewison-
    Carter
Steven Hey
Richard Higgins
Graham Hill
Joe Hill
Jon Hill
Sarah Hill
Tricia Hill
Victoria Hill

Ed Hillan
Samantha Hills
Matt Hinde
Helen Hinds
Leonie Hirst
Stephen Hiscock
Maggie Holland
John Holt
James Holtzclaw
Ben Hopkins
Mark Horstmeier
Philippa Hoskin
Adam Hough
Jim Houghton
Adrian Howard
Catherine Howard-
    Dobson
Suzanne Howe
Steven Howell
Elise Huard
Philip Huggins
George Hughes
Mark Hughes
Jay Humphrey
Caroline Hunter
Andrew Hyams
@IgnoredAmbience
Peter Iles-Smith
Felix Iliff
Mark Iliff
Camilla Imperiali
Olivia Imperiali
Martin Instinsky
Mikaela Irish
Tom Irving
Andrew Jackson
Chris Jackson
Mel Jackson

Stephen Jackson
Simon Jagger
Mike "Withnail"
    James
Richey James
David Jaques
Lyndsay Jarvis
Thibault Jeakings
Ben Jemmett
Bethan Jenkins
Dai Jenkins
Jay Jernigan
Simeon Jewell
Matthew Job
Claire Johnson
Hazel Johnson
Howard Johnson
Matt Johnson
Aidan Jones
Caroline Jones
Lauren Jones
Matthew Jones
Mike Jones
Richard Jones
Karen Joy
Jo Joyce
Alex K
Zeeshan Kadri
William Kahler
Christos Kallinteris
Nancy Kane
Kate Karnage
Joanne Kaye
James Kears-Burke
Russell Keegstra
Danny Keillor
Alex Kelly
David Kelly

Mirren Kelly
Neil Kelly
Sian Kelly
Tricia Kelly
Donald Kennedy
SJ Kennedy
Ida Keogh
Jo Kershaw
Alison Keys
Dan Kieran
Matt Kilcast
Eleanor King
Ian Kirby
Nika Kirch
John C. Kirk
Martin Kirk
Jackie Kirkham
Stephen Kitt
Andreas Kjeldsen
Lars Klawitter
Burkhard Kloss
James Knowling
Simon Koppel
Arec Koundarjian
Alys Kowalik
Martha Krumbach
Beate Kubitz
Neville Kuyt
Myria Kyriacou
Avgi Kyriazi
Pierre L'Allier
Joel Lacey
Ben Laker
Yvonne Lam
Dario Landazuri
Paul Landreth
Alexandra Lanes
Ole Larsen

Samantha Last
Andrew Laver
Gilbert Laycock
Liz Laycock
Ruth Le Ber
Nick Le Fevre
Kieran Leach
Faith Lee
Jonathan Lee
Benedict Leigh
Jacob Lesgold
Robin Levett
Charlie Lewins
Andrew Lewis
Graham Lewis
Kes Lewis
Myz Lilith
Andrew Lillywhite
Matthew Lind
Pete Lindsay
Steven Linnington
David Lloyd
Jonathan Lloyd
Peter Lloyd
Dan Lockton
D Lodge
Craig Lodzinski
Deborah Lofas
Ted Logan
Suzi Long
Philip Lovell
Janet and
    Brendon Lovett
Isaac Lowe
Andy Lulham
Elspeth Luna
Naomi Luxford
Joe Lynch

Mike Lynd
Adam Lyzniak
Tim M
Angus MacDonald
Dagmar Mackett
Russell Mackintosh
Donald Macleod
Laura Magnier
Diarmuid Maguire
Chris Major
Kizzy Makinde-
    Corrick
Hugh Malan
J.A. Malcolm
Ralph Malein
Jessica Maloney
Aditya Mandrekar
Anne "3.1" Maningas
Keith Mantell
Cortney Marabetta
Eric Marcus
James Mardell
Zan Markan
Liz Marley
Jen Marsh
Peter Marshall
Terrance Marshman-
    Edwards
Ciara Martin
Colin Martin
Philip Martin
Adam Martin-
    Lawrence
Richard Martin-
    Nielsen
Lyn Marven
Ross Masters
Katherine Mathieson

David Matkins
Alex Matthews
John Maullin
Thom May
Dawood Mayet
Natasha Mayo
Lucy MBE
James McBride
Chris McCartney
Dave McCormick
Chris McCray
Kat McDonald
Ian McDougall
Anna McDuff
Jeremy McGee
Neil McGovern
Alisdair Calder
   McGregor
Mitch McGregor
Rhydwyn Mcguire
Peter McGurk
Kieran McIlwain
Mark McKeever
Matt McKenzie
Richard McKinley
Mark McMullan
Steve Mcmullen
Iain McSpuddles
Jennifer McWilliam
Tom Mellor-Clark
Daniel Mercer
Minna Meritahti
Kimberley Metcalfe
Earle Meyer
Vladimir Michev
Tom Miles
Steve Milford
Jonathan Millar

Richard Miller
Anne Minter
Claire Miskell
Ian & Debs Mitchell
Louise Mitchell
Peter Mitchell
John Mitchinson
Oliver Monk
Tom Moody-Stuart
Bethany Moore
James Moore
Joseph Moore
Melissa Moore
Zuleikha Moosajee-
   Harrison
David Morgan
Ed Morland
Matt Morris
Clare Morrison
Richard Morte
Cathy Mossman
Dominick Moxon-
   Tritsch
Graham Mulholland
Michael Mullan-
   Jensen
Graham Mullier
Marie Mulligan
Neil Mundy
Dave 'Thadrin'
   Munro
Adam Murphy
Alona Murray
Daniel Murray
Edel Murray
Jon Murray
Sean Murray
Neil Murton

Eleanor Musgrove
Robert Mushett Cole
Hannah Mycock-
   Overell
Naath
Joshua Natzke
Carlo Navato
Matthew Neal
Indranath Neogy
NeonFerret
Katharine Newman
E Nicholls
Jane Nicholson
Jules Nicholson
Kiya Nicoll
Ross Nicoll
Stewart Noble
Ben Norland
Jordan NS
Peter Nuttall
James O'Brien
Ross O'Brien
Kevin O'Connor
Anne O'Hara
Peter O'Neill
Ciara O'Sullivan
Peter O'Connor
Oaf oaf oaf!
Phil Oakes
David Odie
Michael Olivier
Per Olsson Gisleskog
Greg Opie-Martin
James Oprey
Gill Othen
Steve Overall
Jezz Palmer
Ignazio Palmisano

Steven Pannell
Jeff Parke
Tom Parker-Shemilt
Rachel Parkin
Marianne Paterson
Sarah Patrick
Mark Pattison
Gus Paul
Sumit Paul-
    Choudhury
Simon Pawson
Harry Payne
Tim Payne
Christopher Pell
Will Penington
Robert Pennington
Ian Penovich
Kerryn Percy
Neil Perrins
David Perris
Sam Perry
Konrad Petrusewicz
Hywel Phillips
Jonathan Phillips
Sarah Philo
Juliette Pickles
Sarah Pickles
Neil Pickup
Tom Pigden
Eirik Pitkethly
Hiroko Plant
Jonathan Platt
Irene Polderman
Justin Pollard
Steve Pont
Martin Poole
Dave Pooser
David Povall

Catherine Preston
Chloe Prevett
Bronwyn Prew
Barry Price
Clare Pringle
Trevor Prinn
Michael Prior-Jones
Lucy Proctor
Simon Proctor
Lisa Quattromini
Caleb Quilley
Kevin F. Quinn
Giles Radford
Andy Randle
James Ratcliffe
Robin Raven
Stuart Rayfield
Colette Reap
Simon Reap
Gareth Reeve
Rachel Reeves
Julian Regel
Caryl Regnault
Isaac Reid-Guest
Joel Rein
Derek Peter
    Reinhard Hawley
Emma Reiss
A Reynolds
Tina Reynolds
Ian Richards
Stephen Richardson
David Riddell
Jonathan Ridge
Ian Ridley
Jennie Rigg
Lars Rinde
Chiara Riondino

Laura Roberts
Nick Roberts
Paul Roberts
Phil Roberts
Tony Roberts
Giles Robertson
Helen Robertson
Alan Robinson
Clare Robinson
Paul Robinson
Sunil Rodger
Stjohn Roe
Julie Roff
Darren Rogers
Kyle Rogers
Felix Rohrbach
Kinga Rona-Gabnai
Mark Roper
Claudia Ross
Kate Rothwell
Bryan Roughan
Mike Rovardi
Paul Rowell
David Rowntree
Rozasharn
Freddie Ruddick
John Russell
Damien Ryan
Lars S
Matt Sach
Adam Salem
David Salgado
James Salisbury
Jonathan Salisbury
Christoph Sander
Oliver Sander
John Sanders
Louise Santa Ana

Simon Sardeson-Coe
Jack Saunders
Tom Savage
Iain Savill
Bevan Sawatsky
Edward Saxton
Helen Saxton
Burkhard Schafer
Robert Schroeder
Benjamin Scott
Caz Scott
Colin Scott
Fiona Scott
Jenn Scott
John Scott
Manda Scott
Mich Scott
Sarah Scott
John Scott-Roe
Graham Seaman
Julian Self
Filip Selldén
Dick Selwood
Victoria Senior
Keith Sharp
Andrew Shepherd
Sher3ert
Karl Sherratt
Keith Sherratt
Jonathan Shewell-
    Cooper
Graham Shirling
Tim Short
Daniel Shurz
Samuel Sidenbladh
Kevin Sides
Lesley Sigall
Chris Simpson

Ian Simpson
Martin Sinclair
Phillip Skentelbery
Peter Sketch
Åsmund Steen
    Skjæveland
Dennis Skovborg
    Jørgensen
Sadie Slater
Tom Slatter
Paulina Sliwinska
Dermot Smith
Joshua Smith
Mark Smith
Richard Smith
Colin Snodgrass
Timothy Snow
Matthew Somerville
Robin Sonefors
Helen Southall
Richard Speed
Andrew Spencer
Ben Spencer
Jon Spencer-Hall
Dominik Spitzer-
    Wong
Simon Stacey
Rob Stanley
Pete Stanton
Ian Stapley
Oliver Stevens
Craig Stewart
Al Storer
Ian Stott
Leanne Stott
Frederick Stourton
Darren and Ellen
    Strange

Rebecca Strickland
John Styles
David Sullivan
Bethany
    Summerfield
Murali Suriar
Chris Suslowicz
Andrew Sutherland
David Swanson
Mary Sweet
Stephen Sweet
Stephen Swindley
Will Sykes
Gavin Syme
Tim T.
Alex Tarrant-
    Anderson
Iain Tatch
Annie Taylor
Ben Taylor
Deb Taylor
Georgette Taylor
Jack Taylor
Matthew Taylor
Paul Taylor
Phil Taylor
Stephen Taylor
Rob Taylor-Ailes
Edwin ten Dam
Chris Terry
Jamie Thom
Giles Thomas
Jen Thornton
Paula Thurlbeck
Alex Tischer
Deirdre Tobin
Giles Todd
Kiwi Tokoeka

Darren Topham
Greg Toulmin
Mark Townend
Michael Toze
Sarah Travers
Ciaran Treanor
Rose Tremlett
Robin Triggs
Katherine and
    Simon Trill
Kate Trumper
David G Tubby
Andrew Tudor
Andrew Turnbull
Giles Turnbull
Charlotte Turner
Neil Turner
Ian Turton
Kit Turton
Anna Tyler
Albert van Andel
Dawn Van Dyke
Arnoud van Vliet
Adam Vartanian
Paul Vaughan
Edward Venning
Pete Verdon
Marius Verwoerd
Aldo Viale
Bettina Vine
Catherine Virgo
Bella Vivat
James von Simson
Yury Voronin
@vreemt
Marco Vujevic
R W
Andrew Waddie

Essie Wagner
Charlotte Walford
Alex Walsh
Brandon Walts
Joshua Warburton
Bethonie Waring
Anne Warner
Michael Warren
Ben Watkin
Paul Watson
Daniel Weir
Max Werler
Matthew West
Paul West
Luke Westendarp
Christopher Whiffin
Matt White
Lara Whitelaw
Adam Whitford
Peter Whitworth
David Widdick
Filip Wieland
Eliane Wigzell
Sean Wilks
Adrian Williams
Donna Williams
Gareth Williams
Jay Williams
Mike Williams
Nia Williams
Peter Williams
Rachel Williams
Rhiannon Williams
Mark Williamson
Alison Willis
Clara Willmott-
    Basset
Rob Wilmshurst

Charlie Wilson
Chris Wilson
Dale Wilson
Daniel Wilson
Jennifer Wilson
Niall Wilson
Olivia Wilson
Stew Wilson
LJ Winter
Simon Withers
Fabian Woltermann
Michael Wonham
Martin Wood
Tobias Wood
Hamish Woodhouse
Wayne Woodward
Lee Wratten
Chris Wray
Caroline Wren
David Wren
David Wright
Naomi Wright
Black Xanthus
Nuala Yilmaz
Adrian Young
Cathy Young
Will Young
Michael Zahner
Genera Zollinger